The Living Presence

Chiara Lubich

The Living Presence

Experiencing Jesus in the Word, the Eucharist and Our Midst

New City
London   Dublin   Edinburgh

First published in three separate volumes:

The Word of Life as *Parola di Vita*
Città Nuova, Rome 1975 and in English 1981

The Eucharist as *L'Eucaristia*
Città Nuova, Rome 1977 and in English 1979

Where Two or Three as *Dove due o tre*
Città Nuova, Rome 1976 and in English 1977

All three translations revised © New City, London 1996

The Living Presence published in 1997 by
New City, 57 Twyford Avenue, London W3 9PZ

Cover illustration by Anneke Kaai, property of Bouwbureau Braudwij
Cover design by Duncan Harper

British Library Cataloguing-in-Publication Data
A catalogue Reference for this book is available
from the British Library

ISBN 0 904287 55 6

Typeset by Phoenix Typesetting, Ilkley, West Yorkshire
Printed and bound by
BPC Wheatons Ltd, Exeter, Devon

Contents

Preface 7
Introduction 9

The Word of Life 13
The Word of Life and the Fathers of the Church 15
Constantly Being the Word 24
The Effects of the Word 31
The Word Gives Birth to Christ 43

The Eucharist 51
The Eucharist and the New Testament 53
The Eucharistic Celebration in the Life
   of the Church 65
Unity with Christ and with One Another 78
The Eucharist at Work in Us 92

Where Two or three 107
Jesus in Our Midst 109
Being Alone and Being United 119
Jesus in the Midst in the Life of the Community 130
Jesus in the Midst in the History of the Church 140

Preface

Talks given for specific occasions do not always make good books. The writings in this book are an exception. They are packed with remarkable insights, drawn from experience, which have enduring value.

These writings began as talks given by Chiara Lubich to members of the Focolare Movement as part of their yearly programme of meditation upon the deep things of the life in Christ that they share. In a way precisely that specific character is the secret of how this book is able to speak to a much wider audience.

For experience is of its nature specific; it can only be had by particular people, at particular times and in particular places. But at the same time experience tends also to have a dimension that makes it appeal beyond the particular group or individuals who first had it. This is especially true of experiences of God in Christ. In this sense, then, while these writings speak about something that has been tried and tested in the limited confines of the Focolare Movement, they are capable of speaking to many others. There is no need to be a member of the Focolare to appreciate what Chiara Lubich has to say!

The revised edition of these writings is offered, therefore, to all who feel that they can benefit from reflecting upon the presence of Jesus in the Word, the Eucharist and among those who are gathered in his name.

Introduction

The writings in this book – on the Word, the Eucharist and the presence of Jesus among those gathered in his name – deal with three aspects of a mystery, a mystery in the ancient sense of the word of a reality that passes human understanding. As all such mysteries, it can be thought about, discussed and even, within a limited sphere, penetrated by the intellect. But it is always greater than anything anyone can think.

What is the mystery? It is an experience, the experience of a living presence. This presence is One who is more real than any of the things apparent to our everyday senses. It is Christ. Every line in this book speaks about meeting him.

Christ it is who dwells in a person who lives his Word, Christ who is received in the Eucharist and Christ who is the One in the midst of people gathered in his name. But the meeting with him is not merely an intimate, highly personal event. Each of the themes explored in this book has a powerful social dimension. If the Word is lived, it generates community, with a new way of relating to one another, one that values and enhances everything that is human. If the Eucharist is allowed to have its full effect, it brings about the Body of Christ among those who receive the sacramental body, and that means a new way of being together, a social relation that shares in Christ's own way of loving. And if people love one another as Jesus taught, Jesus himself will be found in the heart of their very relationship, the One who unites them, enlightens them and who raises their social relations to a higher, divine, level.

Each aspect of the mystery is in its particular way, therefore, a channel by which the same Christ is communicated. It could be said that they are all about the same thing. It is also true, however, that they are different, and that each of the three is, paradoxically, a preparation for and a fulfilment of the others.

Hence living the Word is both a preparation for receiving Jesus in the Eucharist, because it makes people ready for this meeting with Jesus and, at the same time, a preparation for having Jesus in the midst, since the Word lived enables people to have the kind of love necessary for the presence of Jesus to be among them. But, seen from a different point of view, the Eucharist is, on the one hand, a preparation for living the Word, since it provides fuel for the Christian to live as God commands. While, on the other hand, the Eucharist is a preparation for living with Jesus in the midst, because the Eucharist's primary effect is to generate the Church, to give life to the Body of Christ, and this is lived in its fullness when people meet together with Jesus present among them. Seen from a third angle, however, the presence of Jesus in the midst is a preparation for living the Word, because it gives those among whom the Lord is present the strength, the light and the enthusiasm to live his Word. And this presence is also a preparation for the Eucharist, because it brings about the divine life among people both as a group and individually, so that they are able to receive Jesus in the Eucharist with the best possible attitude as they already find themselves experiencing the essentially eucharisitic effect of being the Church, of being the living Body of Christ, of being, as it were, Christified together.

Thus, since each aspect of the mystery is a preparation for the other, each is in a sense a fulfilment of the other; it concludes what the other begins.

This is not just high-flown theology. It is a matter of daily experience. So the explorations in this book seek more than anything else to communicate an experience. This, therefore, is how they should be understood. All the attempt at accuracy of doctrine is at the service of life. Therefore to understand correctly what is written, the most intelligent procedure is to put it into practice, in a living, day-by-day meditation. For all its value the head can only lead the reader to the edge of the mystery. To enter the mystery the whole of a person's being must be involved.

The full ecumenical import of these writings can be grasped if they are understood in this way. While Chiara Lubich is a Roman Catholic, faithful to her tradition, with an immense love and devotion for her own Church, the experience she shares is one that goes beyond all the barriers of divided Christendom. Indeed, it would be true to say that potentially this experience goes beyond any human barriers at all. For the living discovery of Christ reaches out to the heart of every human heart. He is the One we are made for.

The universality of these writings comes from this simple fact of presenting a way to encounter Christ. In a sense they point to how we can go behind words to the living presence who gives rise to the words which seek to explain, guide and describe the meeting with the One who comes to us. Hence while the author's expressions are indeed often couched in the language and thought patterns of one particular Church tradition, they are a gift offered beyond that tradition. But often too Chiara speaks in an ecumenical manner since her experience, which is so reminiscent to that of the early Christians, is frequently illustrated by the words of the Church's thinkers before its historical divisions of the last thousand years.

This book, therefore, can perhaps best be described as an opportunity open to all. An opportunity to enter into an experience, one capable of transforming individuals and societies: the living presence of Christ.

The Word of Life

The Word of Life and the Fathers of the Church

Let us take a closer look at that priceless treasure which has now been part of the life of the Focolare Movement for thirty years: *the word of life*, the word of God.

But what is the word of God?

I remember one day the answer came to me in a clear and striking way when I read in the Gospel, 'I have made known your name to those whom you gave me from the world. They were yours, and you gave them to me, and they have kept your word. Now they know that everything that you have given me is from you; for the words that you gave to me I have given to them, and they have received them and know in truth that I came from you; and they have believed that you sent me.'(John 17: 6-7) When I read this passage I had the impression in the depths of my soul that the expressions, 'your word', 'everything that you have given me', 'the words which you gave me' and 'I came from you' in one sense meant the same thing, that is to say the words spoken by Jesus were Jesus himself, the Word pronounced by the Father from all eternity.

This was an exhilarating discovery for me, and I wished to have confirmation of it from the Commentary by Augustine, a Father of the Church. This is what he wrote: 'Whatever God the Father has given to God the Son, he gave by begetting . . . for how else should he give any words to the Word, in whom he ineffably spake all things?'[1] We were therefore in unison with St Augustine.

Let us take things in order.

The *word of life*, as all the basic things of our life, has its story.

I was hungry for truth and so I studied philosophy. Even more than that, like many other young people I was searching for truth and I believed I could find it through study. But then came one of the great ideas in the first days of the Movement, which I immediately passed on to my companions; it was this: why should we search for truth, when truth lives incarnate in Jesus, the God-man?

If truth attracts us, let us leave everything, let us search for him and follow him.

That is what we did.

We took the Gospel and we read it word by word. And we found it to be completely new. It shone with Wisdom in every passage. Each word of Jesus was a blazing beam of light: all divine!

This seemed to be the answer to my previous search.

The Gospel could not be compared to any other book because in the Gospel God himself speaks. 'The one who comes from above is above all,' says St John; 'the one who is of the earth belongs to the earth and speaks about earthly things.' (John 3:31)

This is the difference between what we say and what Jesus says: he comes from above, we come from the earth.

His words are *unique*, *eternal*: 'The grass withers, the flower fades; but the word of our God will stand for ever.' (Isa. 40:8)

These words were *fascinating* for us, written with *divine incisiveness*, they possessed a kind of *terrible majesty*,[2] they were *words of life* to translate into life, words that were *universal* in time and space.

In fact, Jesus is risen: he is alive and is present, and this must be our conviction just as it was in the early Church.

And if Jesus is risen and alive, his words, even if they were said in the past, are not just a simple record, but rather words that he speaks today to all of us and to every person in every age.

The words of Jesus!

They must have been his greatest art, if we may use that expression. The Word who speaks in human words: what meaning, what intensity, what emphasis, what tone of voice!

Compared with the Gospel, everything that was not inspired by God seemed *watered-down* to us, even when it had to do with spiritual matters. Even the theories of great thinkers, though they sometimes revealed some partial truth, seemed to melt into *worthlessness*.

We repeated the experience of some of the Fathers of the Church.

Listen to what Gregory Nazianzen says: 'The great word of God overshadows all the persuasive and multiform ways that the human spirit has of speaking, just as the sun which moves in the sky outshines every other splendour.'[3]

And Basil asserts: 'one day arising as from a deep sleep I looked out upon the marvellous light of the truth of the Gospel and beheld the uselessness of the wisdom "of the rulers of this age, who are doomed to perish"[1 Cor. 2:6]'.[4]

Justin, the philosopher, affirms: 'All the good things that the philosophers and lawmakers said were worked out with difficulty, uncovering and contemplating a part of the Word which is Christ, often they also said things which contradicted one another.'[5] And elsewhere he concludes: 'Considering deep within me the words of Christ, I saw that this was the only sure and useful philosophy.'[6]

Thérèse of Lisieux, like us, found the words of human beings inadequate compared with the words of God. This is the reason behind her love for the Gospel: 'Whenever I open a book by a spiritual author, no matter how beautiful or touching, my heart dries up and I can understand nothing of what I read . . . I am rescued from this helpless state by the Scriptures. . . but during meditation I am sustained above all else by the Gospels. They supply my poor soul's every need, and they are always yielding up to me new lights and mysterious hidden meanings.'[7]

And Teresa of Avila says: 'I have always been fond of the words of the Gospels and have found more recollection in them than in the most carefully planned books - especially books of which the authors were not fully approved, and which I never wanted to read.'[8]

Of the various ways in which we came into contact with the word of God, such as the liturgy and in meditation, two marked our initial steps: one was to listen to the word of God within us, which we called *listening to that voice*, and the other was the practice of living a word of God, usually taken from the Gospel, for a set period of time.

In fact, the first focolarine looked with admiration at the

group St Augustine formed with his disciples, and a common expression among them was the saying, *in interiore hominis habitat veritas* – within the human person dwells the truth.

What made the first focolarine say this was the fact that, since they were Christians, the word of God was a reality which had been placed in their hearts ever since they were little and had first come to know Christianity, and which the action of the Holy Spirit had gradually made part of them. And so they constantly encouraged one another with the words, 'Listen to that voice', especially as advice when they had to make a decision.

In fact John says, 'the word of God abides in you.' (1 John 2:14) And also, 'the truth that abides in us . . . will be with us forever.' (2 John 2)

The Holy Spirit, therefore, inspired us not to neglect that source of truth which already was flourishing deep in our souls.

The second way that the Lord showed us how to assimilate the Gospel was *to live the word*.

We would give our attention to a complete sentence of the Gospel, meditate on it, and write a commentary which we would then have approved by the person who represented the Church for us, and we lived it.

The Lord (we understood it much later) was giving us the alphabet, as we called it, that enabled us to know Christ. A few letters and a few rules of grammar are all that is needed in order to know how to read and write, we used to say, but if one does not know them, one remains illiterate all one's life. The few sentences of the Gospel were sufficient to form Christ in us.

This idea of the alphabet is not new, I have discovered. Others have had it before and this makes us feel we are children of the same mother, the Church, and brothers and sisters of the saints.

Bonaventure says: 'The disciples of Christ must study holy Scripture like children learning their ABC . . . who later begin to read one-syllable words, and then to read, and later still to connect the meaning of phrases.'[9]

Gertrude the Great says: 'Place your wonderful alphabet before me . . . Now teach me through experience the glorious Alpha of your beautiful love. Do not hide from me the fruitful Beta of your royal wisdom. Show me with care the single letters of your charity, so that, with my heart's eye purified by the truth, I might penetrate deep down to your most hidden delights, and that I might search, study, learn, know and understand, inasmuch as is possible here in this life, the letters of the heavenly alphabet.'[10]

We lived the word of God. We *lived* it: this is what we felt the Holy Spirit inspired us to do most. It was a voice within us that echoed back the written words: 'be doers of the word, and not merely hearers who deceive themselves.' (Jas. 1:22) And, 'Everyone then who hears these words of mine and acts on them will be like a wise man who built his house on rock.' (Matt. 7:24)

This is what the saints did. Hilary, Bishop of Poitiers, says: 'Everything in the words of God must be accomplished; and all that is said intrinsically demands to be put into practice. The words of God are decrees.'[11]

We did not just live the word of God individually, each one on their own account. The useful experiences, the light we received, the graces that came to us in living it, were shared; they had to be shared, because our spirituality demands that we become holy together. As a result whoever listened benefited and whoever spoke was enriched.

In fact, Maximus, Bishop of Turin, says: 'The nature of spiritual words is such that, when they take effect, the result is of mutual benefit, giving comfort to the person who listens and to the person who speaks.'[12]

And Bernard of Clairvaux, a Doctor of the Church, says this: 'In you, brothers, I really find ears to hear... but I confess that, even while I am speaking, I sometimes have the impression of experiencing the fervour of your devotion. In fact, the more plentifully you suck, the more the Holy Spirit deigns to fill my breast, and the more abundantly he gives me that which I offer you.'[13]

We felt the duty of communicating what we experienced to the others, because we were conscious that in *giving* an experience, it remained and was constructive for our inner lives, whereas if we did not give it, slowly our souls grew impoverished.

We lived the word intensely all day long, therefore, and we communicated the results not only among ourselves, but also to those who joined our first group. It was like a watchword, which everyone wanted to hold on to in order to be certain of being part of the newly-born community.

But what grew out of all this was really something new. In order to understand it well, you have to imagine that before this happy moment when the Holy Spirit enlightened us in such a special way about the word of God, we had not been used to living the word of God like this, applying it to all the circumstances of our lives and sharing the results with one another.

At most, we used to meditate on the word of God, and penetrate it with our minds; we drew up a few points for consideration, and if we were fervent, made a few good resolutions.

Now things were completely different. We carefully examined the word of God in its most varied applications through continuous contact with life, and it brought about a transformation in each individual and in the group. When we were living it, it was no longer 'I' or 'we' who were living, but the word in me, the word in us. And this was the Christian revolution with all its consequences.

We saw clearly that the word was the seed of a tree that blossomed in each individual and in the heart of the community.

Jesus speaks about seeds in the parable of the sower when he explains the growth of the word which falls on different types of ground with varied results. This reality of the seed, which has been so vivid ever since the very beginning of our Movement, reminds us of Isaiah:

> 'For as the rain and the snow come down from heaven,
> and do not return until they have watered the earth,
> making it bring forth and sprout,
> and giving seed to the sower and bread to the eater,
> so shall my word that goes out from my mouth;
> it shall not return to me empty,
> but it shall accomplish that which I purpose,
> and succeed in the thing for which I sent it.' (Isa. 55:10-11)

Outsiders who observed what was happening were astonished, I remember, to find rather than a word of the Gospel that was meditated upon, a living Christian community. And sometimes they asked themselves what strange kind of meditation we had done on the word of God.

The fact of the matter is that the seed is destined to die in order to give life to the tree, just as the word of God is destined to be '*eaten*' in order to give life to Christ in us and Christ among us.

St Jerome expresses this marvellous development magnificently: 'The preaching of the Gospel is the smallest of all the philosophical doctrines. In announcing the scandal of the cross, in fact, it has no other truth than faith in the death of the Lord, God and human. Compare this teaching with the systems of philosophers, with their books and their dazzling eloquence and you will see how the Gospel is the smallest of all the seeds. But those doctrines when they develop themselves, do not show anything living, concrete or vital, but all grow weak and lifeless and rotten: they are like grass and vegetables which wither and die. But the preaching of the Gospel, which seems small at the start, when it develops in the soul of the believer, as in all the world, does not become a plant, but grows like a tree.'[14]

Constantly Being the Word

> *'In the beginning was the Word,*
> *and the Word was with God,*
> *and the Word was God.*
> *He was in the beginning with God.*
> *All things came into being through him.'*
> *(John 1:1-3)*

The Word, who is God, came down among us one day, carried out his mission as redeemer, and then ascended into heaven, to be at the Father's side.

But his real presence has remained in various ways all over the earth: in the Eucharist, in his word, among us when we are united in his name, within us, and in the hierarchy of the Church.

One of the real presences of the Word, who is God, is therefore the word of God.

'I want to tell you about the word of God,' says Augustine. 'What word is it? Where does its greatness lie? "All things were made by the Word". Look at the works and stand in awe of him who did them. "*All things were made by the Word*"!'[15]

Augustine saw clearly the activity of the Word in creation and, therefore, its divine omnipotence and breathtaking height.

The word of God!

'God willed that many things be said and received through the prophets, his servants. But what a huge difference when his Son comes to speak! The Word of God who inspired the prophets, is now here with his very own voice,' says Cyprian.[16]

His words cannot but be 'spirit and life'. (John 6:63) Through them we pass from death to life, and giving life to all things they penetrate everything. 'The word of God is living and active', says Paul, 'sharper than any two-edged sword, piercing until it divides soul from spirit. . . it is able to judge the thoughts and intentions of the heart.' (Hebrews 4:12)

If the word of God is the Word of God, it was logical at the time when the Movement began, as in every age, for the talks containing this word to have had an extraordinary effect on the people who listened, that is to say, for them to have shone with such majesty and splendour as to leave many people convinced and strongly moved to do good.

It was also logical that those who declared that they practised their religion were surrounded by great esteem and veneration.

In reality, we often suffered greatly to hear the word 'sermon' used in a derogatory sense when it should have been an echo of the words of Jesus, a flash of supernatural light, an unction of the Spirit. At times the word sermon had come to mean the same as a lesson that was empty, boring and ineffective. We also observed that many religious people aroused the scorn and hatred of the world not so much because they lived the Gospel, but rather because, with their inconsistent lives, they emptied it of meaning.

This fact made us blush because up to that time we too had certainly been just like those Christians. This realization branded an indelible conviction in our hearts: *first we must live and then speak*. That is how Jesus had acted: he had begun by doing and then he taught.

Besides the Gospel, the Fathers of the Church also followed this line.

John Chrysostom affirmed: 'Jesus said that we must first act and then teach how to act; he places the practice of doing good, before teaching, showing that we can only usefully teach after having first put into practice what we teach, and never otherwise. In another place Jesus says: "Physician, heal yourself." (Luke 4: 23) A person who is not able to regulate his own life well and who tries to teach others, runs the risk of being laughed at by many; what is more, he will not even be able to teach, because his actions witness the opposite of his words.'[17]

To proclaim the word without a living witness was a scandal to pagans just as it is to non-Christians in our own times, leading them to criticize us, just as in early times it led to blasphemy instead of conversion.

In the second letter of Clement of Rome to the Corinthians, we read 'when pagans hear our mouths proclaim God's sayings, they admire their beauty and greatness. But later, when they realize that our actions do not correspond to our words, they change their mind and begin to scoff, saying that Christianity is a myth and a deception.'[18]

Again Augustine says: 'His words remain in us when we do what he has commanded us and desire what he has promised us; however, when his words do remain in our memory, but there is no trace of them in our life and our behaviour, then the branch is no longer a part of the vine, because it no longer draws life from its root.'[19]

The conviction that we first had to live and then speak was so strong among us that we were not satisfied with living the word when there was an occasion to do so, but we nourished ourselves with it *every moment* of our lives. Just as our body breathes in order to stay alive, so our soul in order to live lived the word.

Our living the word in this way was the secret of our renewal and of our Christian revolution.

I have the impression that if each day we were to repeat to ourselves and to those who live with us this idea of putting the word into practice, we would render one of the greatest services to the cause of Jesus.

'Our mind,' says Ambrose, 'should *always* remain with him and never go away from his temple, never be separated from his word. May we always concentrate on reading Scripture, on meditating and praying, so that the word of 'the One who is' may *always* be at work within us.'[20]

If we read some of the writings from the first years of the Movement we can see the Spirit strongly inspiring us in this direction.

This letter of mine dates from 1948. 'We've understood that the world needs to have treatment. . . Gospel treatment, because only the Good News can give it back that life which it is missing. This is why we live the *Word of Life* . . .

'We *incarnate* it in us to the point of being that living word.

'One word would suffice to make us saints, to make us another Jesus.

'In time we will live many words of Scripture so they will remain as an indelible patrimony of our soul.

'*To live the word of life in the present moment of our lives, this is our task.*

'All of us can live it, whatever our vocation, age, sex or

social condition, because Jesus is light for everyone who comes into this world.

'With this simple method we re-evangelize our souls and with them the world . . .

'Try to live it and you will find in it all perfection. Just as each morning you are happy with the sacred Host which you receive without desiring others, in the same way be fully satisfied with this word. You will find, as St Francis did, "the hidden manna of a thousand fragrances." In this way and only in this way: *by practising the truth, we love!* Otherwise love is empty sentimentalism. But true love is Jesus Christ, the Truth, the Gospel!

'Let us be living Gospels, words of life, each of us another Jesus! And we will really love him, and imitate Mary, the Mother of the Light, of the Word: the living word.

'We have no other book except the Gospel, we have no other knowledge, no other art.

'This is where Life is.

'Whoever finds it does not die.'

Now, as the Movement is spreading so widely, we would like people to be able to say of us too: 'Let what you have heard from the beginning abide in you. If what you heard from the beginning abides in you, then you will abide in the Son and in the Father.' (1 John 2:24)

Since then there have been three daily communions for the members of the Movement: communion with Jesus in the Eucharist, with the word of life, and with our neighbour.

This love for the word was so constant and important as to make us say that the word of God was our clothing.

The following passage was written in 1950:

'For us, for each one of us, the word of life is the dress, the wedding dress of our soul which is the spouse of Christ. It is for us what the habit is for religious orders. Someone who is a religious is sanctified only if they remain within their vocation. They cannot change it. They cannot change their habit. For us the habit is an inner one . . .'

Besides this, God had shown Mary to us, Mary the Christian *par excellence*, completely clothed with the word of God, indeed, the word of God personified.

We saw that this was true of every member of the Movement, it was at once what they were and what they ought to be.

Therefore we gave the same importance to communion with the word of God as to communion with the Eucharist, and of course with our brother or sister, with whom it was our daily duty to share our experiences of the word of life.

The Fathers of the Church, who reflect the mentality of the early Church, often put the Body of Christ and his word on the same level.

Clement of Alexandria pointed out that we must nourish ourselves on the seed of life contained in the Bible as we do on the Eucharist.[21]

'My refuge is the Gospel, which for me is like the flesh of Christ,' says Ignatius Martyr.[22]

Jerome said: 'We eat his flesh and drink his blood in the divine Eucharist and also in the reading of the Scriptures.'[23]

And Gregory Nazianzen compared the reading of Scripture to the eating of the paschal lamb.

Tertullian in the *Book of the Resurrection*, compared the word that gives life, to the flesh of the Son of God.

And the wise Origen wrote that the word that nourishes souls is in a way another body with which the Son of God has clothed himself . . .

And Augustine had this to say: 'Tell me brothers, what do you think has greater value, the word of God or the Body of Christ? If you want to answer in truth, you must agree that the word is not less than the Body of Christ. Therefore, if when we are given the Body of Christ we are very careful that nothing falls from our hands to the ground, in the same way we must be careful when the word of God is given to us not to let it slip away from our hearts, because we are speaking or thinking about something else. You are no less guilty if you receive the word of God negligently than if through carelessness you let the Body of Christ fall to the ground.'[24]

And to conclude this comparison between the word of God and the Eucharist, I will refer to what the Second Vatican Council says: 'The Church has always venerated the Holy Scripture as it has venerated the very Body of Christ, never failing, especially during the Sacred Liturgy, to nourish itself on the bread of life in the banquet of the word of God and of the Body of Christ, and to offer this bread to all the faithful.'[25]

There is nothing left to do but to go on along this way, holding on tight to the word. Like the Eucharist, it too has multiplied the presence of Jesus here on earth.

This gives us great comfort, but it also involves a greater responsibility if we want to present ourselves to the world as genuine followers of Jesus.

What more could we want? What could be greater than this?

The Effects of the Word

If we observe the people who live the word of God, we see at once a great variety of effects that the word brings about in them. Each soul is like a crystal with many facets to which the light of the word, wherever it touches, gives various shades of colour. There are an infinite number of situations in which people can find themselves: there are an infinite number of reactions that the word, the Word of God, provokes in each person.

If we wanted to list the fruits it produces, we could go on forever. But let us give a few examples.

The word makes you 'live'

The first impression of anyone who is in contact with a part of the Movement, where the word is lived as it should be, that is, both by individuals and by the community, is that this is a place where people live. You can tell by the light that shines on the face of whoever welcomes you, by people's gestures, by their readiness to be of service, by a kind of rejuvenation that the word causes, not only in the soul, but even in the body. This happens because the word is *life*.

Athanasius expresses this fact well when he comments on the verse from the Psalms: 'Your word gives me life.' He says, 'Nothing else makes a rational soul *live* in its specific life like the word of God.'[26]

The word makes you free

Another effect, which is characteristic of the word, is that it makes you free. In fact the Gospel says it: 'The truth will make you free.' (John 8:31)

The truth makes us free because if, before all our thoughts, affections and our will, our first interest is the word, everything that happens becomes secondary. Misfortunes are secondary, graces are secondary, tragedies are secondary, the adventures of love are secondary, health is secondary, sickness is secondary - everything is secondary.

What counts for us is whether or not in all these events we have lived the word.

If we have done this, we feel a great freedom, freedom from other people, freedom from happy or unhappy circumstances, freedom from ourselves, freedom from the world that tries in a thousand different ways to mar the peace of the kingdom of God within us.

The word guarantees happiness

'The Gospel,' Pope Paul VI says, 'guarantees our happiness... but it changes the nature of this happiness. It does not consist in transitory goods, but in the kingdom of

God: in vital communication with him.'[27]

You experience this happiness which is as serene as the dawn of a sunny day, soft and gentle and yet at the same time full, and it makes your soul exult in a simultaneous *Te Deum* and *Magnificat*. It is unique. It cannot be mistaken for anything else. Those who have experienced it think back to it in other moments of their lives, because it is a shining white mountain peak, like the memory of a little Mount of Transfiguration in the soul.

The word converts

Coming to know the Movement and conversion of life are usually one and the same, and we see marvellous things happening.

There are people who were attached to the world, to their ego and their position in life, and who now seek the last place; there are others, who were unable to utter a single word even before a tiny group of people, and who now reveal their discovery to the crowds. Experience has also shown that when people who suffer from temptations against chastity live this ideal, they feel relieved and transformed, especially during the first months as if all their problems had disappeared. The money given for the poor or for the works of the Movement is often the fruit of the savings of someone who has worked hard to acquire it. We meet people full of zeal for God's cause after years of discouragement, now, as they say, that they have 'found the answer'. And love, which is the basis of our spirituality, restrains anger to such a degree that often you might never realize during someone's lifetime that anger could have been their main vice.

Similarly, we could list thousands of other effects, like those which Gregory the Great recognized as fruit of the word: 'Through the power of the divine word,' he said, 'a proud person receives humility and a timid person self-confidence, a lustful person is cleansed in his efforts to be chaste, and a greedy person is tempered and held back from burning ambition; a discouraged person stands straight again with righteousness and zeal, a hot-headed person is restrained from excitement and hasty action. In this way, God with his waters, irrigates all things: He adapts the power of his word to individuals, according to their varied behaviour, so that each one finds in His word exactly what he needs to give him the tiny seed of that virtue which is necessary for him.'[28]

The word purifies

Once we have placed our entire past in the mercy of God and have begun again to live the word, we have the impression - and it is a reality - that the word has purified everything within us. 'Whoever hears the word [and therefore puts it into practice] is already purified.'(cf. John 15:3)

Ambrose wrote this too: 'They are words, it is true, but they purify.'[29]

The word gives life to the most varied vocations

When the word is put into practice, it gives rise, in the midst of the Christian community, to individual vocations: to virginity, to the priesthood, to the religious life, to marriage (a real little Church because it reflects the life of the whole Church), to be lay people, who, though remaining immersed in the world with all its complications, want to make God prevail over every other ideal.

The word produces the hatred of the world and the holiness of the disciple.

When the word is lived by the disciples of Jesus, it does not leave outside observers indifferent. Often it happens that this extremely new life arouses relentless criticism. In fact, I would say that if the world did not rebel against a life lived according to the Gospel, the disciples of Christ, who should be in complete contrast to it, could not qualify as 'not of this world'. And the criticism sometimes reaches the point of hatred. This gives us the great martyrs of the Church and also the little martyrs who, from time to time, we also find in our Movement, who are troubled and at times overwhelmed by the lack of understanding of those who ought to understand them most.

At the same time, if the evangelical life causes misunderstanding and hatred, it is the way which leads to holiness.

We cannot speak about people who are still alive, but we can affirm with certainty that many members of the Movement who have already passed to the next life, should be considered as little saints. This is shown by the way they faced very grave situations, painful sicknesses, and by the conversions which took place around their beds as they approached the next life. Their own deaths give witness to it, and so do their funerals, which are usually permeated by an atmosphere of paradise. When people who attend those funerals go back home they often say: 'It seemed as though we were at a wedding feast.'

We repeat with the Curé of Ars: 'In my cemetery [and ours is as vast as the world itself] saints are at rest.' Hatred, therefore, and holiness – these are two typical effects of those who live the word. But let us hear how Jesus himself puts it: 'I have given them your word, and the world has hated them because they do not belong to the world, just as I do not belong the world. . . . *Sanctify* them in the truth; *your word* is truth.' (John 17: 14-17)

The word makes you see the truth

Sometimes, when speaking with children and young people who live the word, one feels like saying: the Holy Spirit is speaking in you. They give the clear impression that they can *see*. How true are St Augustine's words: 'Now you are believers, if you persevere in faith you will become seers. . . and you will know the truth.'[30]

The word brings comfort

How often the saints, and we Christians, hard pressed by pangs of doubt, or by a decision we have to take, or of some misfortune that comes unexpectedly, take the book of God and open it to find comfort! We repeat what is written in the Book of Maccabees: 'we have as encouragement the holy books that are in our hands.' (1 Macc. 12: 9)

The word gives us joy

Above all, the word of God brings joy. All public events of the Movement are characterized by joy.

Ambrose says: 'A person well instructed and intent upon the word of God will do nothing unreasonable which would cause him to be sad, but rather, always master of his own actions, he will know how to preserve the unshaken joy of a clear conscience.'[31]

The word produces works

The words of God also yield abundant fruits, and works blossom. For years now, more as spectators than as actors, we have been admiring the great number of works which the members of the Movement carry out. It is such a spontaneous flourishing and such a vast one that in itself it witnesses the Work of God.

John of Damascus says: 'Like a tree planted beside a stream of water a soul which is watered with Holy Scripture becomes prosperous and is always adorned with green leaves, that is, with works which are of beauty in God's eyes.'[32]

The word gives wisdom

The word of God is wisdom. And wisdom is light for every situation: when you need to clear up doubts, to speak out for justice or to know how to govern well, or to be enlightened about God's plans for individuals or for the world.

Let us hear what Paul writes to Timothy: 'Continue in what you have learned and have firmly believed, knowing from whom you learned it, and how from childhood you have been acquainted with the sacred writings that are able to instruct you . . . All Scripture . . . is useful for teaching, for reproof, for correction and for training in righteousness, so that everyone who belongs to God may be proficient, equipped for every good work.' (2 Tim. 3: 14-17)

The word preserves us from human worries

We see that whereas many people are all tied up in worldly affairs, those who live the word are calm and not afraid of anything.

John Chrysostom confirms it: 'The sea is raging and you will calmly sail over it; your pilot is the reading of the Scriptures, and your rudder will not be broken to pieces by the temptation of worldly affairs.'[33]

The word obtains everything

When you live the word, you obtain everything. I do not want to exaggerate, but I am certain that each day all over the world, where people live the word, they obtain countless graces. I say it for the glory of God, because I know the countless times it has happened to me too.

But it is logical. Jesus says: 'If you abide in me, and my words abide in you, ask for whatever you wish, and it will be done for you.' (John 15: 7)

The word brings about union with God

When people begin to be able to live the word of God, they become aware of communion with Jesus as a fruit within their soul. This is shown by the fact that they speak to him with great ease, they call upon him in moments of need, they enjoy his presence in the depths of their soul; in fact, they feel that the interior life has been born in their hearts and is grafted on to the vine which is Christ.

The word of God, having become part of us, places our soul under the action of the Holy Spirit, in a vital union with Jesus. It is not a case of an exterior contact or exterior encounter, but of a profound communion of life.

The word gives hope of eternal life

The word of life leads and has led the entire Movement to the conviction that, just as we see the evangelical promises fulfilled one by one, so one day, through the word, the gate of heaven will be opened for the soul.

In fact, Jesus says: 'Very truly, I tell you, whoever keeps my word will never see death.' (John 8: 51)

The word makes us one

The word of God is what has bound us together since the early times when we were all very close, and it is what binds us together now, though we may be far away from one another, overseas. It is a light imperceptible to the senses and unknown to the world, but which is dearer to God than any other thing. Each one of us can be another Jesus: a living word of God.

I wrote in 1948: 'Let's be united in the name of the Lord, living the word of life which makes us *one* . . .

'I was thinking about how plants are grafted together: the two branches are stripped of their bark, and through contact between the two *living* parts they become one.

'When can two souls be perfectly one? When they are *living*: that is, when they have stripped off all that is human, and through living the word of life, incarnating it, they become *living words*. Two *living words* can be perfectly one. If one of them is not living, the other cannot unite with it.

The further on I go, the more I see the beauty of the word of life! It is the little pill which contains in concentrated form all that Jesus brought to earth: the Gospel message.'

Whoever does not live the word causes division

Whoever does not live the word of God, carries everywhere an atmosphere that is merely of the world: such a person does not leaven the mass, but rather depresses it to the point of becoming the cause of friction or disagreement.

This is what Cyprian feared, when, in his treatise *De Unitate* he speaks especially about the unity of the Church, but he does not fail to keep on urging us to live the Gospel, since it is precisely because the Gospel is not lived that there are schisms in the Church.

The word brings about a complete change in mentality

What the word of God brings about is a complete change of mentality. It injects the sentiments of Christ into the hearts of everyone: Europeans, Asians, Australians, Americans, Africans, as they face circumstances, individuals and society. The word makes each citizen of the world a citizen of heaven, with a new nature.

Paul says: 'Be renewed in the spirit of your minds and clothe yourselves with the new self.' (Eph. 4: 23)

The word makes each soul a heaven

To talk of our souls and the souls of our brothers and sisters who shared the same ideal, in the beginning we used the word heaven: the *heaven of my soul*, the *heaven of your soul*.

Now, at a distance of time, intuition tells us that the word *heaven* was a meaningful one, because Jesus says: 'Those who love me will keep my word, and my Father will love them, and we will come to them and make our home with them.' (John 14: 23)

We could go on forever. To sum it up, the life of the word gives human beings a complete re-evangelization of their way of thinking, of willing, of loving. The Gospel, the code of life, becomes incarnate.

The Gospel is not a book like any other. Wherever it takes root it creates the Christian revolution, because it lays down laws not only for the union of the soul with God, but also for the union of people among themselves, be they friends or enemies. It states as its supreme command unity among all, the testament of Jesus carried out at least within the social framework in which Christians who live the word are involved.

And wherever one of these Christians lives, even the desert flowers.

The Word Gives Birth to Christ

Now we may ask ourselves, how were we able to penetrate the word of God, to understand it in a way that made it appear new to us and full of vital, revolutionary force?

We can say now for certain that it was through a special grace, a grace that taught us how to establish the presence of Christ between souls and how to live this presence in a deep way.

This is the way God acted: with his own method of teaching he first called our attention to a few *words* that may seem easier. But he had a very definite reason for choosing those words. In general they were words which had to do with love: 'Love your neighbour as yourself', 'Love one another', 'Love your enemy', 'Love . . .', always love.

We understood the reason behind this choice afterwards: whoever loves acquires light because the fruit of love is inner enlightenment.

But that is not all: the love God puts in the soul is supernatural, it is the participation of our love in the love of God, and therefore by its very nature it is mutual. Through mutual love the Lord gradually accustomed us to welcoming his presence among us. And his presence influenced our understanding of his words. He was the teacher who taught us how to understand his words. It was a kind of explanation, worked out not by a teacher of theology, but by Christ himself.

Anselm, a doctor of the Church, says: 'One thing is having ease in speaking and splendour in one's words, and another thing again is entering into the veins and marrow of the heavenly words and contemplating, with the most pure eye of your heart, the deep hidden mysteries. One cannot obtain this in any way from the doctrine or learnedness of the world, one obtains it only with purity of mind through the teaching of the Holy Spirit.'[34]

The presence of Jesus among us brings us his spirit.

On the other hand we recall that one of the first pages of the Gospel that we read was the testament of Jesus (cf. John 17). This was a very important event. We still remember clearly how, as we passed from one word to the next, each one seemed to be illuminated and then we understood how someone was telling us, 'Look, in school you must learn many things, but the summary of it all is this . . . sanctify them in the truth . . . that all may be one . . . you will have the fullness of joy . . . you will be one as I and the Father are one . . .' The testament of Jesus appeared to us to draw together the whole Gospel in a synthesis. We understood this in a way that could not have been so clear except through a special grace. Once we penetrated this, in the way that God wanted and in as much as God wanted, it was easier for us to understand the rest of the Gospel.

Often we give this example: imagine that the Gospel is like a plain, a large tract of land on which all its words are written; at the end of the land is the testament of Christ which is the synthesis of the whole Gospel. The Lord, teaching us the core of Christ's testament, unity, to which all the evangelical truths are linked, had, as it were, cut a hole into the ground so that we could dig beneath and understand the rest of the Gospel from inside, grasping each word at its root in its truest meaning.

After five or six years of living the different words of the Gospel it became clear to us that they all resembled one another: there was something they all had in common. Each one had as much value as the other, because the effects which they produced in the people who lived them were identical. For example, if we had to live the word, 'Whoever listens to you listens to me' (Luke 10:16), we did not wait to put it into practice just when we ran into a bishop or a superior. Our entire life, every second of our existence, was obedience to what the priests had taught us in catechism and to what we had learned from God directly and then submitted to be approved by the Church. So living this word was equivalent to living all the other words, such as those that tell us to do the will of God, or to love God, or to love our neighbour. Everything therefore was simplified.

Once we had reached this point it might have seemed superfluous to continue with the practice of looking each week at particular one word of life, except that - and this can be a common experience if we correspond to grace - God works on souls and sometimes sends such sublime gifts of light as to give the impression of receiving a deeper understanding of the Gospel.

Under the influence of these graces you discover in the Gospel, for example, that the whole of the life of Jesus is directed towards the Father, and you read the Gospel again in a new light and give your own life in the same orientation.

Then may come the graces of darkness and obscurity, which are like hell, and you doubt everything. What you doubt is the *logic* of the Gospel. You say to yourself – or rather some devilish source suggests: 'If you love you will *see* again, and you will find that yourself drawn back into the *system*,' into the supernatural life, which in that moment appears to you as something dangerous in which you lose your freedom – therefore: 'Stop. Do not love and you will be yourself.' The devil will do everything to keep you from loving. But if you resist ,and do exactly the opposite of what the temptation says, an even deeper vision of the Gospel opens before the soul. You rediscover it as the unique book of life and you understand that you will never be able to comprehend 'the breadth and length and height and depth' of the word of God (cf. Eph. 3: 18).

In this way the Gospel remains the eternal book of your spiritual nourishment.

Now let us move on to another point.

The word of God! The word of God is not like other words. Not only can we listen to it, but it also has the power of bringing about what it says.

And since the word is Christ, *it gives birth to* Christ in our soul and in the souls of the others.

Even before we live the word, if we are Christians, we have grace in us, and therefore the life of Christ in us, and along with this grace there is without doubt also the light and love of God, but they are rather closed in as though in a chrysalis. When we live the Gospel love radiates light, and the light makes love grow: the chrysalis begins to move and then later a butterfly emerges. The butterfly is the little Christ who begins to be formed in us and then grows more and more, so we become ever more filled with him.

Our ideal teaches us this. This is what the word of God wants to do in us: to form Christ in us so that our preparation for the next life is no more than the culmination of a life lived for those days, for that hour, for the true Life.

That the word gives birth to Christ in us has been said by many - popes, saints, Fathers of the Church.

Pope Paul VI gave a magnificent description of what the word produces, and of the way in which it is to be received. He suggests a method which is the same as that used in our Movement. He says: 'How does Jesus become present in our souls? This is how: through the communication of the word by which the divine thought is passed on, the Word, the Son of God made man. We could assert that the Lord becomes incarnate in us when we let this word come to live within us.

'When we hear the Gospel explained, every Christian should be sure that he makes at least one precious point his own. Then when he goes home . . . all during the week that follows, he should nourish himself on this substantial spiritual food: the word of the Lord.

'Therefore, first of all listen, then . . . keep this word . . . Not only a passive act of acceptance is needed but also an active reaction, a reflection. You must meditate on the word . . .

'There is a third moment. The word must be turned into action and guide our life. It must be applied to our lifestyle, to our way of living, judging and speaking . . .

'In this way the Christian life is shown to be extremely attractive.'[35]

Ignatius of Antioch had a splendid idea of the word. He felt that since we have come from the mind of God we are destined to return there, as *words of God*. Writing to his followers in order to stop them preventing his martyrdom, he said: 'I do not wish you to seek that which pleases man but that which pleases God, by whom you have been accepted. For I shall never have such another opportunity as this to attain to God . . . , if you keep silent (and allow me to go to martyrdom) *I will become a word of God*.'[36]

James affirms: 'of his purpose he gave us birth by the word of truth, so that we would become a kind of first fruits of his creatures.' (James 1: 18)

And then there is a saying of Jesus in the Gospel that makes us stop and think. When the apostles approached him and tell him that his mother and brothers were outside waiting for him, Jesus replied: 'My mother and my brothers are those who hear the word of God and do it.' (Luke 8: 21) Could it be possible that Jesus allows us in some way to be *his mother?* Yes, he himself said it.

We can give birth to Christ in souls, as a mother gives birth, through the word.

And the fact that we can be the mothers of Jesus is clearly stated by Gregory the Great: 'We must know that one who is a brother or sister of Jesus through faith, becomes his mother through the word. If, through your words, you bring to life in your neighbour's soul a love for the Lord, you almost generate the Lord, because you bring him to life in the heart of the one who hears your word, and you become the mother of the Lord.'[37]

In the same way St Paul felt very strongly that he had become the father of his followers through the word which he had sown in their hearts: 'For though you might have ten thousand guardians in Christ, you do not have many fathers. Indeed, in Christ Jesus I became your father through the gospel.' (1 Cor. 4: 15)

Augustine saw the Church as born from the word of God: 'The very Apostles on whom the Church was founded, following Christ's example preached the word of truth and gave birth to the churches.'[38]

The Church, therefore, is born precisely through the proclamation of the word.

In its turn the Church is a mother and gives life to souls through the gift of the word and through Baptism.

We can say the same for our Movement. It came into being through the word that Jesus sowed in our hearts, and in its turn it has become the mother of many souls, bringing them to life by planting the word in human hearts: the word, which is not just a simple idea, but is 'spirit and life'. (John 6: 63)

Therefore, the word of God gives life to Christ in individuals, in communities and in Churches. This is why St Clement of Alexandria could say: 'whoever obeys the Lord and through him follows the Scriptures which have been given to us, is fully transformed in the image of the Master; he reaches the point of living like God in human flesh. But you cannot reach these heights unless you follow God in the way he leads you; and he leads only through the divinely inspired Scriptures.'[39]

To place ourselves in contact with the word of God is therefore to put ourselves into vital contact with Christ, to absorb his life. For this reason, echoing the Song of Songs,

'Let him kiss me with the kisses of his mouth' (Song of Songs 1: 1), we too can assert that each moment in which we live the word is like a kiss on the mouth of Jesus - that mouth which only spoke words of life. He (who is the Word) communicates himself to our souls. And we are one with him! Christ is born in us.

Gregory of Nyssa expresses the same idea: 'Now the source of the living water of the word is the mouth of the Spouse, from which the words of eternal life proceed, filling the mouth of him who draws there . . . therefore, you must put your mouth close to the water if you want to drink from the source: now the source is the Lord who said: "Let anyone who is thirsty come to me, and let the one who believes in me drink"', [John 7: 37] and this is the reason why your soul desires to put its mouth close to the mouth which is the source of life, saying, 'Kiss me with the kiss of your mouth' [Song of Songs 1: 1]; and he who possesses this life-spring for everyone, and who wants everyone to be saved, does not allow anyone of those who are saved to be left without this kiss, this kiss which becomes the purification from every sin.'[40]

After everything we have said about the word, the only thing left to do is to draw this single conclusion: How much longer have we still to live? Let us live the word in each present moment always more intensely so that we, too, can be for the world and for the glory of Christ a *God in human flesh*.

The Eucharist

The Eucharist and the New Testament

Jesus Eucharist, what presumption, what audacity it is to speak of you, you who, present in churches throughout the world, know the secrets, the confidential words, the hidden problems, the sighs of millions of people, the tears of joyous conversions known only to you, the heart of hearts, the heart of the Church.

We would not speak of you at all, and would avoid breaking the reserve due to a love so high, so lofty as yours, if it were not that our own love seeks to overcome every fear and yearns to go a little beyond the veil of the white host, of the wine of the golden chalice.

Forgive our daring! But love wants to know in order to grow in love, and so as not to end this earthly journey without having discovered, at least a little, who you are.

And yet we have to talk about Eucharist: because we are Christians, and in the Church, our mother, we live and bring her the ideal of unity.

Now, no mystery of faith has as much to do with unity as the Eucharist. The Eucharist opens up unity and brings out all its content. In fact, it is through the Eucharist that there comes about the consummation of the unity of human beings with God and with one another, and of the unity of all the cosmos with its Creator.

God made himself a human being. And so we have Jesus on earth. He could do everything. But the logic of love demanded that, once he had taken a step like this from the Trinity to earthly life, he should not stay just for thirty three years, even though with a divinely exceptional life like his, but that he should find a way of staying in every century, and especially of being present in every point of the world, in what was the highest moment of his love: sacrifice and glory, death and resurrection. And he did remain. With his divine imagination he invented the Eucharist.

It is his love which reaches the extreme.

Thérèse of Lisieux put it like this: 'O Jesus, let me say, in overflowing gratitude, let me say that your love reaches madness.[41]

The institution of the Eucharist

But let us hear how it all took place. Matthew, Mark, Luke and Paul talk about it.

Luke says: 'When the hour came, he took his place at table, and the apostles with him. He said to them, "I have eagerly desired to eat this Passover with you before I suffer; for I tell you, I will not eat it until it is fulfilled in the kingdom of God . . .

'Then he took a loaf of bread, and when he had given thanks, he broke it and gave it to them, saying, "This is my body, which is given for you. Do this in remembrance of me".

'And he did the same with the cup after supper, saying, "This cup that is poured out for you is the new covenant in my blood".' (Luke 22:14-20)

If Jesus had not been God, I do not know how in so few solemn words he could have presented realities that are so new, unpredictable, and fathomless that they cast you into ecstasy, because, once they are understood a little, human nature cannot withstand such things.

Jesus, you are there the only one who knows everything, the only one who realizes that your gesture ends centuries of waiting, and who looks upon the infinite consequences of what you are doing to carry out that divine plan foreseen by the Trinity from all eternity: the Church which has its beginning on earth and which penetrates deep into the future depths of the kingdom. I repeat, if you had not been God, how could you have talked and acted in such a way?

But something of what your heart felt in that moment does shine through to us in the words, 'I have eagerly desired', and there is an immense happiness, 'before I suffer', and there is the meeting of joy with the cross and the link between the two, because what you were about to do was to be your testament and a person's testament is only valid after death. You left us an inheritance beyond human measure; you left us yourself.

Pierre Julien Eymard, founder of the Blessed Sacrament Fathers, says: 'Jesus Christ, too, wants to have his memorial . . ., his masterpiece to make him immortal in the hearts of his followers, as an unceasing reminder of his love for humankind. He will be its inventor and craftsman, he will consecrate it as his last testament, and his death will be its life and its glory . . . this is the divine Eucharist.'[42]

Then Jesus 'gave thanks'.

Eucharist means 'thanksgiving' and the supreme thanksgiving was the one offered to the Father for having watched over and saved the human race by intervening in the most marvellous ways.

And he took the bread and the cup, and said: "This is my body, which is given for you. Do this in remembrance of me . . .

'And he did the same with the cup after supper, saying, "This cup that is poured out for you is the new covenant in my blood.'

This is the Eucharist.

It is the miracle.

According to Thomas Aquinas the Eucharist is the greatest of Jesus' miracles.[43] In fact, as Pierre Julien Eymard says, 'It exceeds all the others in its object, and is superior to all for its duration in time. It is the permanent incarnation, the perpetual sacrifice of Jesus, it is the burning bush that is always aflame on the altar; it is the manna, the true bread of life, that comes down from heaven each day.'[44]

'These mysteries,' as Ignatius of Antioch says, 'crying to be told, but wrought in God's silence.'[45]

And the Second Vatican Council affirms that 'in the most blessed Eucharist is contained the whole spiritual good of the Church, namely Christ himself, our Pasch and the living bread which gives life to men through his flesh - which is vivified by the Holy Spirit and vivifies, and gives life to men.'[46]

From the Old to the New Testament

Jesus celebrates his Passover like a banquet. In every home, the evening meal is the time of the deepest intimacy, of brotherhood, and often of friendship and celebration.

The banquet at which Jesus presides is celebrated like the Jewish Passover, and as such it contains in a summary form the entire history of the people of Israel.

Jesus' last supper is the fulfilment of all God's promises.

The 'elements' of the new supper are full of the meaning they have taken on in the Old Testament. The bread, a gift of God and an indispensable means of life was a symbol of communion, a reminder of the manna. The wine, which the Book of Genesis calls the 'blood of grapes' (Gen. 49:11), was offered in sacrifices (cf. Exod. 29:40) and it was the symbol of the joy of the Messianic times (Jer. 31:12). The chalice was a sign of participation in joy and of acceptance of affliction and it called to mind Moses' Covenant (Exod. 24:6). And bread and wine were promised by Wisdom to her disciples (Prov. 9: 1-6).[47]

Like the father of a family, Jesus, in his gestures and in the 'prayer of blessing' repeats the Jewish rite. But in this banquet there is a tremendous difference and novelty compared with the Hebrew Passover. Jesus' supper is celebrated within the context of his passion and death, and in the Eucharist he anticipates, in a symbolic and real way, his sacrifice of redemption. Jesus is the priest of this sacrifice, Jesus is its victim.

Pope Paul VI spoke in these terms on Maundy Thursday 1966: 'We cannot forget that the Supper... was a commemorative rite, it was the paschal banquet, which had to be repeated each year in order to transmit to future generations the indelible memory of the liberation of the Jewish people from the slavery of Egypt . . . That evening, Jesus replaced the Old Testament with the New: "This is my blood", he said, "of the New Testament . . ." (Matt. 26: 28); with the old historical and figurative Passover, he links up his own Passover and makes it follow on from the old one. His Passover is historical too and is definitive, but it is also figurative and points towards another final event, the final parousia (the second coming).'[48]

The words of Jesus, 'I tell you, I will never drink of this fruit of the vine until that day when I drink it new with you in my Father's kingdom' (Matt. 26:29), which the famous exegete Benoit translates as 'an appointment in Paradise',[49] give the Eucharist the characteristic of a banquet that will reach its total fulfilment after our resurrection.

For Athanasius, however, already in this life we can participate in communion with the risen Christ. Athanasius, referring to this Passover of the New Testament, says: 'We do not approach a temporal feast, my beloved, but an eternal and heavenly. Not in shadows do we shew it forth, but we come to it in truth!' He also says that we no longer celebrate this feast by eating lamb's meat, but 'we eat the Word of the Father'.[50]

For Athanasius, to eat the bread and wine which have become the body and blood of Christ is to celebrate the Passover,[51] that is, to relive it. In fact, the Eucharist is the sacrament of communion with the paschal Christ, with Christ who has died and is risen and has passed on (Passover = Passage), has entered a new phase of his existence, the glorious phase at the right hand of the Father. As a result, to receive Jesus in the Eucharist means to participate already here on earth in his life of glory, in his communion with the Father.[52]

The bread of life

John has his own way of describing Jesus Eucharist. Already in the sixth chapter of his Gospel he recounts that the day after Jesus had multiplied the loaves, in the great speech at Capernaum, he says: 'Do not work for food that perishes, but for food that endures to eternal life, which the Son of Man will give you.' (John 6:27)

Shortly afterwards Jesus presents himself as the true bread come down from heaven, which must be accepted through faith: 'I am the bread of life. Whoever comes to me will never be hungry, and whoever believes in me will never be thirsty.' (John 6:35)

And he explains how he can be the bread of life, 'and the bread I will give for the life of the world is my flesh.' (John 6:51)

Jesus already considers himself bread. And so this is the ultimate reason of his life here on earth. To be bread so as to be eaten, to be eaten so as to communicate his life to us.

'This is the bread that comes down from heaven, so that one may eat of it and not die. I am the living bread that came down from heaven. Whoever eats of this bread will live forever'. (John 6:50-51a)

How shortsighted we are compared to Jesus.

He, the infinite who comes from eternity, has protected a people with miracles and graces, and built up his Church, and he moves on towards eternity where life is never lacking.

We, at most, limit our gaze to today or maybe tomorrow, in this our brief existence, and at times we fret over trifling things. We are blind. Yes, blind, often we Christians too are blind. Perhaps we do live our faith, but we are not fully conscious. We do understand Jesus in a few things he says which have to do with our consolation or guidance, but we do not see the whole of Jesus. 'In the beginning was the Word,' then creation, then the incarnation, then almost a second incarnation through the Holy Spirit in the Eucharist, which serves as our viaticum, our food for the journey through this life to the next, then the kingdom with him, divinized by his person, which is in his body and his blood which have become Eucharist.

If we view reality in this way, everything assumes its rightful value, everything is projected towards the future that we shall reach, if already here on earth we try to live, insofar as we are able, in the heavenly city, in a commitment of love towards God and all humankind, like Jesus who went through the world doing good.

What an adventure life is if it has this outcome!

The pharisees were arguing, and Jesus answers, explains and reaffirms, and finally he says: 'Those who eat my flesh and drink my blood abide in me, and I in them. Just as the living Father sent me, and I live because of the Father, so whoever eats me will live because of me.' (John 6:56-57) '. . . abide in me, and I in them' – here unity is consummated between Jesus and the human person who is nourished with him, bread. In this way the fullness of life, which is contained in Jesus and which comes to him from the Father, is transmitted to human beings. With this the indwelling of Jesus in a human being is achieved.

Albert the Great writes: Christ 'embraced us with too much love, because he united us to himself so much that he is in us, and he himself penetrates into our innermost parts . . .

'Divine love produces ecstasy. It is right to call divine love ecstasy, because it transposes God into us and us into God. The Greek word ekstasis means transposition. In fact, he [Jesus] says: "Those who eat my flesh and drink my blood abide in me, and I in them" [John 6:57]. He says, "They abide in me", that is to say, they are placed outside themselves; and "I abide in them", that is to say, I am placed outside myself.

'And this can be done by his . . . charity, which penetrates into us . . . and draws us to him. Not only does it draw us to him, it brings us into him, and he himself penetrates into us right to the very marrow of our bones.'[53]

In this stupendous chapter of John's Gospel, Jesus affirms: 'And the bread that I shall give for the life of the world is my flesh' (John 6:51) and also, 'Those who eat my flesh and drink my blood have eternal life, and I will raise them up on the last day'. (John 6:54)

'For the life of the world.' Therefore, the Eucharist already serves in this world to give life. But what is life? Jesus told us: 'I am the life' (cf. John 11:25; 14:6). This bread nourishes us with him, already here below.

'And I will raise them up on the last day.' The Eucharist also gives life for the next world. But what is the resurrection? Jesus told us: 'I am the resurrection' (cf. John 11:25).

The resurrection is Jesus who begins in us his immortal life, the life that does not end with death. Even if the body is corruptible, life, which is Christ, remains in the soul and in the body as the principle of immortality.

The resurrection is a great mystery for all who reason with human standards.

But there is a way of living in which the mystery becomes less incomprehensible.

By living the Gospel viewed from the perspective of unity, we experience for example that in carrying out the new commandment of Jesus, mutual love leads to fraternal unity among people, and this exceeds even natural human love. Now this effect, this achievement is the result of our doing the will of God. Jesus knew, in fact, that if we responded positively to his immense gifts we would no longer be his 'servants' or his 'friends', but his 'brothers and sisters' and brothers and sisters to one another, because we would all be nourished with his very own life.

John the Evangelist uses a helpful image to indicate this different kind of family: the image of the vine and the branches (John 15). The same sap, or we could say the same blood, the same life, that is, the same love which is the love with which the Father loves the Son, is communicated to us (cf. John 17:23-26), and circulates between Jesus and us. Therefore we become one flesh and one blood with Christ, and so it is in the truest and deepest supernatural sense that Jesus calls his disciples 'brothers' after his resurrection (John 20:17). The author of the Epistle to the Hebrews confirms that the risen Jesus 'is not ashamed to call them brothers and sisters'. (Heb. 2:11)

Now, as this family of the heavenly kingdom has been built, how can we think of death as putting a sudden end to the work of God, with all the painful consequences this would imply? No. God would not face us with an absurd separation. He had to give us an answer. And he did give it, in revealing the truth of the resurrection of the body. This truth almost seems no longer a dark mystery of faith to the believer, but rather a logical consequence of Christian living. It brings us the immense joy of knowing that we shall all meet again along with Jesus who united us in this way.

The Eucharist in the Acts of the Apostles

Revelation also mentions the Eucharist in the Acts of the Apostles. . .

The early Church was extremely faithful to Jesus in carrying out his words, 'Do this in memory of me'.

Regarding the first community of Jerusalem, in fact, we read that: 'They devoted themselves to the apostles' teaching and fellowship, to the breaking of bread and the prayers' (Acts 2:42). And talking about Paul's apostolate: 'On the first day of the week, when we met with for the breaking of bread, Paul was holding a discussion with them . . . Then . . . after he had broken bread and eaten, he continued to converse with them until dawn'. (Acts 20:7,11)

The Eucharist in the epistles of Paul

Also in his first letter to the Corinthians, Paul shows his ardent and firm faith in the body and blood of Christ, with the words: 'The cup of blessing that we bless, is it not a sharing in the blood of Christ, and the bread that we break, is it not a sharing in the body of Christ?' (1 Cor. 10:16), and he goes on to describe the effect that this mysterious bread has in the person who receives it, saying: 'Because there is one bread, we who are many are one body, for we all partake of the one bread.' (1 Cor. 10:17)

One body!

This is how John Chrysostom comments: 'We are that self-same body. For what is the bread? The Body of Christ. And what do they become who partake of it? The Body of Christ: not many bodies, but one body. For as the bread consisting of many grains is made one so that the grains nowhere appear... so are we conjoined both with each other and with Christ.'[54]

Jesus, you have a great plan for us, and you are carrying it out through the centuries. It is to make us one with you so that we may be where you are. You came from the Trinity down to earth, and it was the will of the Father that you return, but you did not want to go back alone, you wanted to go back together with us. This, then, is the long journey: from the Trinity to the Trinity, passing through the mysteries of life and death, of suffering and glory.

How wonderful that the Eucharist is also 'an offering of thanks'. Only through the Eucharist can we ever thank you enough.

The Eucharistic Celebration in the Life of the Church

The Eucharist, too, throughout the centuries, has its story of an ever-deeper understanding of this mystery which, more than any other, is the 'mystery of faith'.

All things have worked together to reveal the infinite wealth the Eucharist contains – the Eucharist 'all God and all man', as Catherine of Siena says. Everything that has ever happened, happy events and sad ones, the Ecumenical Councils, the ever-vigilant, infallible magisterium of the Church, the experience of the saints, heresies, wars and bitter negations have all contributed, in the plan of God, towards opening up the eyes of the faithful to continually new aspects of the mystery of the Eucharist.

God the Father sent thousands of angels from heaven, encircling his beloved Son who had remained among us in an excess of love. He made everything tend towards this, so that as the sun rises dimly at dawn and gradually increases its effects of light and heat until noon draws near, so too Christians could better and better understand him who remained among us and what effects he brings for each individual and for humankind.

This is not the place to give a full account of those events, but I shall mention some, so as to praise God, and also because everything, anything that has to do with him whom we love, is of enormous interest to us.

The eucharistic celebration in the early Church

Ever since the Church existed, the Eucharist has always been its heart. . .

If we ask ourselves what was the focal point for the first generation of the Church, we must answer that it was the eucharistic celebration. In the works of the apologists, of the apostolic fathers, and in the Acts of the Martyrs, all the doctrinal and vital aspects of the Eucharist are emphasized.

In the year 155 Justin described the liturgical celebration as follows: 'And on the day called Sunday there is a meeting in one place of those who live in cities or the country, and the memoirs of the Apostles or the writings of the prophets are read as long as time permits. When the reader has finished, the president in a discourse urges and invites [us] to the imitation of those noble things. Then we all stand up together and offer prayers . . . On finishing the prayers we greet each other with a kiss. Then bread, and a cup of water and mixed wine are brought to the president of the brethren and he, taking them, sends up praise and glory to the Father of the universe through the name of the Son and of the Holy Spirit, and offers thanksgiving at some length that we have been deemed worthy to receive these things from him. When he has finished the prayers and thanksgiving [Eucharistic Prayer], the whole congregation present assents saying 'Amen'. When the president has given thanks and the whole congregation has assented, those whom we call deacons give to each of those present a portion of the consecrated bread [eucharistized food] and wine and water, and they take it to the absent.'[55]

And shortly afterwards, we already find in Justin an expression of exceptional value regarding the real presence: 'This food we call Eucharist . . . is the flesh and blood of that incarnate Jesus.'[56]

Justin also maintains the objective aspect of sacrifice in the Eucharist, while emphasizing its new character. There is no longer room for the bloody material sacrifices of the Old Testament. The Eucharist represents the long-awaited spiritual sacrifice, since the Word of God himself is its victim.

The Eucharist also strengthens brotherly love. In fact, immediately after the 'distribution of the consecrated elements' [bread and wine], Justin writes, 'those who prosper, and who so wish, contribute, each one as much as he chooses to do. What is collected is deposited with the president, and he takes care of orphans and widows, and those who are in want on account of sickness or any other cause, and those who are in bonds, and the strangers who are sojourners among [us], and briefly, he is the protector of all those in need.'[57]

Already in the Didache they said that the eucharistic bread is regarded as a symbol of unity among brothers and sisters who make up the Church. 'As this piece [of bread] was scattered over the hills, and then was brought together and made one, so let your Church be brought together from the ends of the earth into your kingdom.'[58]

Ignatius of Antioch, around the year 100, describes the Christian community gathered around the bishop and already structured: 'You should all follow the bishop as Jesus Christ did the Father. Follow, too, the presbyters as you would the apostles; and respect the deacons as you would God's law. Nobody must do anything that has to do with the Church without the bishop's approval. You should regard that Eucharist as valid which is celebrated either by the bishop or by someone he authorizes.'[59]

Many martyrs of the early apostolic communities united their personal sacrifices with the Eucharist. Polycarp of Smyrna, for example, tied to the stake, prayed as follows: 'God . . . of all creation . . . I bless you because you have seen fit to bestow on me this day and this hour, that I may share, among the number of the martyrs, the cup of your Anointed [Christ] and rise to eternal life both in soul and in body, in virtue of the immortality of the Holy Spirit.'[60]

Irenaeus maintains that God became a human being so that we might become children of God and sees the Eucharist as containing the principle of the resurrection of the flesh: 'so also our bodies, when they receive the Eucharist, are no longer corruptible, having the hope of the resurrection to eternity.'[61]

In these very valuable testimonies, for the most part from direct disciples of the apostles, the following elements are therefore emphasized: Christ in the eucharistic celebration as the centre of the community, the real communion with the body and blood of Christ, the Eucharist as a sacrifice, Christians realizing that they form one single body through the Eucharist, the communion of material goods, the necessary unity with the bishop, the connection between one's personal sacrifice and the eucharistic sacrifice, and the Eucharist as the cause of the final resurrection.

We also note that the liturgical celebration usually takes place on 'the day of the Lord', in memory of Christ's resurrection, and that from the start it has the aspect of a sacred rite, though it also maintains an intimate character. We already find here a distinct framework, though not a rigid one, made up of readings, prayers, the presentation and consecration of the bread and the wine with water, the communion of those present and those absent.

This framework was to remain unchanged until the peace of Constantine (313 A.D.), with a tendency towards an ever-increasing ritualization.

The golden age of liturgy in the East and in the West[62]

Then the golden period of liturgy begins both in the East and in the West. It lasted from the year 300 to approximately 900 A.D. The Fathers of the Church deepened their understanding of the eucharistic celebration in various aspects, especially as the actualization of the passion, death and resurrection of Jesus, and they explained how the faithful should participate in this celebration with the offering of their own self and the life of charity.

During this period we see the rise of great liturgical communities around the patriarchal sees. The celebration no longer has the intimate aspect of a supper, but becomes a ceremony that is solemn in proportion to the understanding of the greatness of the rite.

A deep theological maturity and spiritual wealth are expressed in the 'eucharistic prayers' or canons, which become fixed and obligatory. Even though they are said by the bishop or by a priest appointed by him, they are always an expression of the entire ecclesial community, and this is the meaning behind the use of the plural 'we' in the prayers.

In the variety of their individual characteristics we find, in all the eucharistic prayers, a few essential parts that remain constant: a) the thanksgiving and praise to the Father for having sent Christ to carry out the salvation of the human race; b) the memorial of the last supper, which renders present the offering of Christ, to which the entire Church associates its own offering; c) the invocation to the Father to send the Holy Spirit to consecrate the bread and wine and sanctify the assembly of participants; d) the remembrance of the saints in heaven, which expresses communion with the entire Church and intercession for the entire world.

The instructions that follow on from the Second Vatican Council have added, to the 'Roman Canon', three other 'Eucharistic Prayers', all taken from the liturgy of this golden period.

The Eucharist in the West during the Middle Ages

The fundamental aspect of the Eucharist had been explained and consolidated. Now it was necessary for another aspect to be emphasized: the real presence of Jesus and his personal relationship with each one of us.

In manifesting divine things, God's providence puts anything and everything to use.

Jesus is no less misunderstood in the Eucharist than when he was here on earth.

The great schism of the East and political changes, also influenced people's concept of a liturgical celebration.

The celebration in this period lost many aspects that once

characterized it as being communitarian and belonging to the people. The eucharistic prayer was recited in silence, communion given under the species of bread alone, the number of private masses increased, the faithful more and more gave up going to communion and there was too much emphasis on the priest . . . For some allegorists the celebration of the Mass came to be transformed into a performance of the passion and death of the Lord with extremely dramatic gestures and ceremonies.

Along with the liturgical crisis that we have described there was a dogmatic crisis, which went so far as to deny the presence of Christ in the Eucharist.

But then came the triumph of the Holy Spirit who makes everything work together for the good of the Church. The Church experienced a reaction of faith in the real presence of Christ in the Eucharist, and with this a devotion for the Eucharist in itself was born; and so there came into existence the feast of Corpus Christi, Benediction, adoration and processions with the Blessed Sacrament.

People found adoration to be their most fulfilling form of eucharistic worship, and Thomas Aquinas became the theologian and hymn writer who acclaimed the personal presence of Christ, truly God and truly human, in the Eucharist.[63]

From the Council of Trent to the present-day liturgical renewal

We come now to the period around 1500, the time of the Protestant Reformation, which challenged the adoration of the Eucharist and the sacrifice of the Mass.

The Holy Spirit, through the Council of Trent, forcefully affirmed the truth of the real presence and of the sacrifice of Christ in the Mass.

Regarding the real presence, the Council of Trent teaches: 'in the beautiful sacrament of the Holy Eucharist, after the consecration of the bread and wine, our Lord and Saviour Jesus Christ, true God and true man, is contained truly, really and substantially under the appearance of the objects that the senses can perceive. Therefore our Saviour is not only present according to his humanity at the right hand of the Father, after his natural mode of existence, but at the same time he is present in the sacrament of the Eucharist also by that form of existence which is possible to God, though we can hardly express it in words. With thoughts enlightened by faith we can reach it, and we must believe it with the greatest constancy'.[64]

And regarding the Mass as the sacrifice of Christ: 'by means of the eucharistic mystery, the sacrifice of the cross, achieved once on Calvary, is marvellously symbolized, continually recalled to memory, and its saving virtue is applied to the remission of the sins which are daily committed by us'.[65]

Over the last four centuries the eucharistic mystery has been understood more and more deeply, always, however, in the sense of adoration and communion, and communion is also seen more as an adoration of Christ who is present, than as a participation in the eucharistic banquet. A series of manifestations of personal love for Jesus in the Eucharist developed, such as the Forty Hours devotion, the visit to the Blessed Sacrament, the Eucharistic Congresses. There has been a flowering of religious congregations and institutes dedicated to adoration of the Blessed Sacrament, ranging from the

Blessed Sacrament Fathers to the spiritual families of Charles de Foucauld.

These religious practices have kept the truths of faith and Christian commitment so alive that they have created masterpieces of sanctity in many people.

The Eucharist in our times

And now we come to our own times.

The Church, which contains all things and gives value to all things, through its Magisterium restores the balance with respect to certain aspects of the liturgy that were less clear and less popular, though also valuing things that the faithful already understood.

Pope Pius X's invitations to the faithful to receive frequent communion and to give communion to children are the first signs announcing a new era. The liturgical renewal which began to develop in Belgium, and then in Germany, drawing on the sources of the liturgy of the primitive Church, and the works of the Fathers and Scripture, led to a rediscovery of the theological and pastoral values of the Eucharist.

In fact, the necessity of living like the early Christians in the catacombs during the persecution in Germany, made Christians joyously re-live the early eucharistic liturgies.

In the Encyclical *Mediator Dei* (1947) Pope Pius XII gave a summary that reconciles both old and new in the Church, especially regarding the liturgy of the Eucharist.

More recently, with the Second Vatican Council and with the Encyclical *Mysterium Fidei* (1965) of Pope Paul VI, all the various aspects of the celebration of the Eucharist are emphasized once again: the memorial, the sacrifice of Jesus and of the Church, and the banquet of communion with Christ and with our brothers and sisters.

The celebration of the Eucharist tends towards simpler and more intimate forms in which the people participate; it reflects the commitment of charity and communion which so well answers the demands of our modern world.

The Second Vatican Council says: 'At the Last Supper, on the night he was betrayed, Our Saviour instituted the eucharistic sacrifice of his Body and Blood. This he did in order to perpetuate the sacrifice of the cross throughout the ages until he should come again, and so to entrust to his beloved spouse, the Church, a memorial of his death and resurrection: a sacrament of love, a sign of unity, a bond of charity, a paschal banquet in which Christ is consumed, the mind is filled with grace, and a pledge of future glory is given to us.

'The Church, therefore, earnestly desires that Christ's faithful, when present at this mystery of faith, should not be there as strangers or silent spectators. On the contrary, through a good understanding of the rites and prayers they should take part in the sacred action, conscious of what they are doing, with devotion and full collaboration. They should be instructed by God's word, and nourished at the table of the Lord's Body. They should give thanks to God. Offering the immaculate victim, not only through the hands of the priest but also together with him, they should learn to offer themselves. Through Christ, the Mediator, they should be drawn day by day into ever more perfect union with God and each other, so that finally God may be all in all.'[66]

In reading these passages that have to do with liturgy today, I began to understand the answer to a question that I had often asked: What is it that particularly characterizes those focolarini, who, after years of life in common, with a communion of goods and the fullness of brotherhood with their fellows, become priests?

And the answer was hard to find, because what characterizes them is too simple a thing.

Now I feel I have understood this: they are priests as the Church wants priests to be today.

Love has led them to break down every barrier, no matter how slight, that divided them from their brothers and sisters, and so they celebrate the Eucharist either within the small family of the focolare or in the big meetings (Mariapolises, Congresses, Day Meetings) made up of thousands of people, and they are already united with them in the name of Jesus, as is required.

In fact, in the introduction to the new Italian Missal we read: 'From the moment they meet, Christians from different places and environments must recognize that they are brothers and sisters. Christ present in their midst creates their unity. In fact, he said: "Where two or three are gathered together in my name, there I am in the midst of them".' (Matt. 18:20)[67]

The rite is simple and the atmosphere is a family atmosphere. The Eucharist is not just the priest's business, but everyone's. Those who have to read the various scripture passages prepare themselves, songs are chosen, including the entrance song which expresses the joy of the community assembled together; people make spontaneous offerings and prayers of petition and thanks. And the priest is there, at the centre, to renew, in the name of Christ the sacrifice of the cross.

And the presence of Jesus 'batters down' hearts, and people often cannot keep back their tears, and they make the most difficult resolutions, as if they were alone with Jesus on the altar. A child once told me, 'During Mass I had an experience. I was alone with Jesus alone'. This signifies that the community was one soul with the priest and with Christ on the altar, and nothing disturbed it.

Then we receive communion in deep silence.

The Eucharist is at the centre, at the climax of our meetings: we need only think how everything else can be considered as a preparation for this personal meeting with Christ, and that almost everyone present goes up to receive communion.

And at the end, the assembly is overwhelmed by a wave of joy; a witness to its unity with the risen Christ.

Then, once the Eucharist is over, almost as an extension of it, priests and faithful go off to bring charity, all day long, into homes and offices and gatherings. Here communion continues and brings liberation, for the development of humankind, in thousands of different circumstances all over the world, is a duty, an obligation, if we want to go on loving as Christ loved.

This is the people of God that has become more fully of God, where the communion of goods takes place silently, but constantly and increasingly, serving thousands of needs; where communion with Christ grows through living his Word, and hearts are aflame with eagerness to evangelize.

These are our priests, completely one with the people of

God, representatives of the people at the altar, vicars of Christ the head of his body, Christ himself in the holy memorial.

Our priests are nothing other than priests! And what an extraordinary adventure that is!

Unity with Christ and with One Another

Having read Scripture and explained a little of what it has to say about the institution of the Eucharist, and having also meditated on the liturgical and dogmatic developments concerning the Eucharist, could give us the impression of having said everything.

But what depths there are in the words of God! They contain God himself.

The Eucharist unites us to Christ

Let us try to see what the difference is between the union with God that the Eucharist achieves and the union that is the effect of other sacraments.

With the other sacraments, we are joined to Jesus through each sacrament's own proper 'virtue', which means through the specific grace of each sacrament.

For example, the sacrament of matrimony gives the grace to live united to Christ in married life.

In the Eucharist, instead, we are united with Jesus himself substantially present, given that in the Eucharist, as John says, we eat his flesh and drink his blood (cf. John 6:53-56).

Baptism, which uses water to signify our being washed from original sin and other sins, is the sacrament of our new birth. This is something personal, and it happens once in a lifetime.

The Eucharist is a form of nourishment. And people take nourishment each day; nourishment is for the maintenance of life and its intensification.

Thomas Aquinas says: '. . . consider the effect of this sacrament in the manner of its giving, namely of food and drink. And so this sacrament does for the life of the spirit all that material food and drink does for the life of the body, by sustaining, building up, restoring and contenting.'[68]

And he also says: 'Just as material food is so necessary for life that one cannot live without it . . . so too spiritual food is necessary for spiritual life, and spiritual life cannot be maintained without it'.[69]

Thomas Aquinas also says that the one who gives life (and likewise Christ in baptism) makes the one who receives life (a human being) in his or her own image, but the giver does not assimilate the receiver into his or her own substance.[70]

The Eucharist, instead, achieves a union of the faithful with God that goes far beyond what is achieved by baptism: it brings about a substantial assimilation.

Of course, all this has to be understood in a way which respects the distance between Creator and creature. It is not a fusion between the communicant and Christ: there is a mystical assimilation which is spiritual but real, and which permits us to speak of 'body', of one body.[71]

In the Decree of the Second Vatican Council *Lumen Gentium* we read that '. . . the sharing in the body and blood of Christ has no other effect than to accomplish our transformation into that which we receive.'[72]

This can be demonstrated by the highest levels of mystical experience, by the transforming union which certain saints reached precisely through holy communion. It is the nuptial character of the sacrifice of the covenant between Christ and his Church, which is also experienced in the union between Christ and the soul.

Having said this, we can understand the extraordinary affirmation of Thomas Aquinas: 'The proper effect of the Eucharist is the transformation of man into God':[73] divinization.

When we read the works of the Fathers and saints, the reality of the Eucharist and its effect on those who receive it with the correct dispositions, seem strikingly new.

We had some insight into this in 1961, when I gave a talk to the first Focolare International School and said: 'God became a human being in order to save us. But, once he was a human being, he even wanted to make himself food so that, by nourishing ourselves on him, we might become other Christs. Now, it is one thing to see Jesus (as we would have, had we lived in his times), and quite another to repeat Jesus in our being: to have the capacity to be another Jesus here on earth. And the Eucharist has this very aim, to nourish us on Jesus in order to make us other Jesuses, because Jesus loved us as himself '.

We Christians have said and heard too many words, but we have often understood too little of Christ's love for us. 'As the Father has loved me, so I have loved you' (John 15:9). That word 'as' is really true. That is the way we are loved. And so we are other Christs, through the Eucharist. But do we realize it? If we did, the world would have changed by now.

Jesus Eucharist, give me the grace, in reading the words of the Fathers of your Church and the words of your saints, to make you known at least a little. This is the anxiety that assails me at the moment, I almost feel anguish at my inadequacy, my incapacity to express that 'something' you made me feel beside you, because it is too great. May the Holy Spirit make up for this. No, may he himself do everything. He has a great deal to do with the Eucharist.

He can light up the illumination beneath the words of the Fathers and saints, and can stir hearts and open up our eyes to our destiny and to Jesus' love for us which goes beyond all the adjectives we know.

Here is what we find in Cyril of Jerusalem: 'for in the figure of bread this Body is given to you, and in the figure of wine this Blood, that by partaking of the Body and Blood of Christ, you may become of one body and blood with him.'[74]

We can speak of being one flesh and one blood not because there is a physical union but because of the union of our persons with the glorified body of Christ which is present in the Eucharist and which is given life by the Holy Spirit. We are therefore really one flesh but in a new, mystical sense of the word.

Cyril carries on: 'For when this Body and Blood become the tissue of our members, we become Christ-bearers and as the blessed Peter said 'partakers of the divine nature'. (2. Pet. 1: 4)[75] And Leo the Great says: 'Our participation in the body and blood of Christ causes us to be transformed into that which we receive and with all fullness we carry, in our spirit and in our flesh, he in whom we are dead, buried and risen.'[76]

And also Augustine, almost as if hearing a voice from

above, writes: 'I am the food of full-grown men. Grow and you shall feed on me. But you shall not change me into your own substance, as you do with the food of your body, instead you shall be changed into me'.[77]

Albert the Great, a Doctor of the Church, in various texts writes: 'This sacrament transforms us into the body of Christ, in such a way that we become bone of his bone, flesh of his flesh, member of his members'.[78]

'Each time two things unite in such a way that one is completely transformed into the other, the one which is more powerful transforms the weaker into itself. Therefore, since this food has a strength that is more powerful than those who eat it, this food transforms those who eat it into itself.'[79]

'Those who have received him [John 1:12] in the sacrament, eating him in a spiritual way, become one flesh with his son and so they are and they call themselves sons of God.'[80]

'The body of the Lord, in this act of generation, is almost like a seed which through its virtue attracts man to itself transforming him into itself.'[81]

'What thanks we owe to Christ, who with his vivifying body transforms us into himself, so that we become his holy pure and divine body.'[82]

Now let us look at the writings of some saints. If you take them on their own they might seem exaggerated, sentimental, crazy, but the Fathers confirm what they say and confirm that they are saints.

Thérèse of Lisieux: 'And now it was not a question of looks, something had melted away, and there were no longer two of us – Thérèse had simply disappeared, like a drop, lost in the ocean; Jesus only was left, my Master, my King.'[83]

But this ought not be just an isolated event reserved for extraordinary people. It should be and it should become the common experience of Christians, if before receiving communion they fulfil all the required conditions that we shall speak about later.

Some members of the Focolare Movement are witnesses of this: since they lived intensely all that was required for the Eucharist to produce its full effect, God revealed to them that they were identified with Christ, and, therefore they uttered the word 'Abba - Father' which the Holy Spirit put on their lips, and they felt themselves immersed in the bosom of the Father.

Anselm Stolz, in fact, in his book *The Doctrine of Spiritual Perfection* says: 'In the Eucharist there is achieved sacramentally the highest possible association with Christ, in the sense of a complete transformation of our sinful being into the glorified being of Christ . . . In sacramental mode Christ lifts those who are assimilated in form to himself out of the confines of time and conducts them before the face of the Father . . . Participation in the Eucharist gives the believer his personal 'rapture' out of this world. At this stage he is led by the Son to the Father in the region of the angels, and in union with the Son he is able to stand before the Father, and addresses him as Father.'[84]

Thérèse writes: 'My heaven is hidden in the host where Jesus, my spouse, hides himself out of love . . . What a divine moment when you, O my beloved, in your tenderness come to transform me into yourself! This union of love and rapture sublime, "this is the heaven that is mine!"'[85]

'Jesus,' Thérèse also says, 'each morning transforms a white host into himself in order to communicate his life to you.

What is more, with a love that is greater still, he wants to transform you into himself.'[86]

And Pierre Julien Eymard: 'It is an ineffable union which comes right after the hypostatic union . . . Why did Jesus Christ want to establish such a union with us? In order to console us with his friendship, and enrich us with his graces and his merits. Above all, with his union of life, he wanted to deify us in himself and thus fulfil his heavenly Father's desire of crowning him [Jesus] also in us, the members of his mystical body.'[87]

The Eucharist and the resurrection of the flesh

Now let us go on to look at another effect on people, an effect that the Eucharist produces in those who receive it fulfilling the necessary conditions. We have already mentioned this before: the Eucharist is the cause of the resurrection of the body.

And since the times we are living in are so lacking in faith, or have altered the genuine faith in such a bizarre way, we shall go back to the Fathers, to the great men and women of the past, or to the Pope to see how they interpreted or interpret the words of Jesus, which in themselves are already so clear . . .

Let us hear what Irenaeus says: 'For when the mixed cup and the bread that has been prepared receive the Word of God, and become the Eucharist, the body and blood of Christ, and by these our flesh grows and is confirmed, how can they [the Gnostics] say that flesh cannot receive the free gift of God, which is eternal life, since it is nourished by the body and blood of the Lord, and made a member of him?'

And he continues, 'Just as the wooden branch of the vine, placed in the earth, bears fruit in its own time – and as the grain of wheat, falling into the ground and there dissolved, rises with great increase . . . so also our bodies which are nourished by the Eucharist, and then fall into the earth and are dissolved therein, shall rise at the proper time, the Word of God bestowing on them this rising again, to the glory of God the Father. It is he who indeed grants to what is mortal immortality, and gives to the corruptible the gracious gift of incorruption, for God's power is made perfect in weakness.'[88]

Justin, who agrees with Irenaeus of Lyons and Ignatius of Antioch on the idea that the Eucharist is a pledge of immortality and resurrection, according to some of his commentators, 'speaks as if already here in this life the Eucharist makes our bodies immortal and effectively begins the resurrection'.[89]

Origen, too, affirms: 'he gives to him that eats of it a share of its own immortality. For the Word of God is immortal.'[90]

Thomas Aquinas writes: 'and it is right that we attribute this effect to the sacrament of the Eucharist, because, as Augustine says, the Word revives souls, but the Word made flesh vivifies bodies. Now in this sacrament not only is God the Word present with his divinity but he is also present in unity with his flesh. Therefore it is the cause not only of the resurrection of souls, but also of bodies'.[91]

Pope Paul VI, in his Easter message 1976, said: 'Christ the Lord is truly risen . . . We also, brethren and sons and daughters, we also will rise! . . . if with a pure and sincere heart we have prepared for Easter, that is if we have been nourished on the Body and Blood of Christ which he offers us in the

Eucharist, for of the one that is fed with this vital food he said: "I will raise him up at the last day".' (John 6:54)[92]

The Eucharist and the transformation of the cosmos

But the effect of the Eucharist in people goes further. Paul says: 'The whole creation waits with longing for the revealing of the children of God; for the creation was subjected to futility, not of its own will but by the will of one who subjected it, in hope that the creation itself will be set free from its bondage to decay and will obtain the same freedom of the glory of the children of God' (Rom. 8:19-21).

This means that all that has been created, in some way, is called to glory. Jesus, who dies and rises, is certainly the true cause of the transformation of the cosmos.

But, since Paul told us that we human beings complete Christ's passion (cf. Col. 1:24) and that nature awaits the revelation of the children of God (Rom. 8:19), God also expects the contribution of people who have been 'christified' by his Eucharist to bring about the renewal of the universe. Therefore we could say that by means of the eucharistic bread, the human being becomes 'eucharist' for the universe, in the sense that together with Christ he or she is the seed of the transfiguration of the universe.

In fact, if the Eucharist is the cause of humankind's resurrection, could it not be that the human body, divinized by the Eucharist, is destined to decay under ground to contribute towards the renewal of the cosmos?

Can we not say, therefore, that after our death, together with Jesus, we are the Eucharist of the earth?

The earth eats us as we eat the Eucharist; not, therefore, to transform us into earth, but to transform the earth into 'new heavens and new earth'.

It is fascinating to think that the bodies of our Christian dead have the task of co-operating with God in the transformation of the cosmos. And deep affection and veneration is born in our hearts for those who have preceded us. This gives us an even better understanding of the age-old veneration for those whom we call the dead – especially the bodies of saints – but who are already being born, in the cosmos, to a new life.

The Eucharist redeems us and makes us God. We, with our death, contribute with Christ to the transformation of nature. The upshot is that nature is the continuation of Jesus' body. And in any case, when Jesus became flesh, he took on human nature, in which all nature converges.

The Eucharist and communion with our brothers and sisters

Here we have a second wonderful effect of the Eucharist; not only does it produce those divine, extraordinary fruits we spoke about in individuals, but as a true 'sacrament of unity', it also produces unity among people. This is logical. If two are like a third, two persons are like Christ, they are like one another.

The Eucharist produces communion between us. This is splendid and, if humanity were to take it seriously, it would result in a paradise beyond our dreams. Because, if the Eucharist makes us one, then it is logical that each person treats the others as brothers or sisters. The Eucharist forms the family of the children of God, who are the brothers and sisters of Jesus and of one another.

In the natural family itself there are rules which, if brought onto a supernatural level and applied on a vast scale, would change the world.

In natural families everything is shared in common: life, home, furniture . . . A family has its intimacy, its members know about each others' situations because they have communicated them to one another.

The members of a family go out into the world bringing the warmth of the home and they can be useful to society, if they are honest and they come from a healthy family.

A family is happy when it gathers round the table or sings or prays together.

If the family is one of the most beautiful works of the creator what will the family of God's children be like?

In the East the value of eating together was strongly felt. Not only does Jesus want his closest followers around him at the last supper, but in passing his own chalice around to his disciples and breaking his bread to distribute it to them, it is as if he wants to clasp his loved ones even closer to himself, almost to unite them to his person.

These acts of Jesus are external signs of the Eucharist as the sacrament of unity.

Then what is wonderful about Jesus' banquet is that he raised that supper to something infinitely higher. In fact, in uniting Christians, through the Eucharist, to himself and to one another in a single body, which is his body, he gives life to the Church in its deepest essence: the body of Christ, fellowship, unity, life, communion with God . . .

Therefore the Eucharist actualizes the Church where people meet together to partake in the eucharistic banquet, and it makes present not just a part of the Church, but the whole Church. It is the whole body of Christ present in one given place, as we see from Paul's letter: 'To the Church of God that is in Corinth'. (1 Cor. 1:2)

The Eucharist also renders all the members of the mystical body present, beyond the limits of distance and death, because the distances of space and time are overcome in the glorious Christ who is present there.

Lumen Gentium affirms: 'When, then, we celebrate the eucharistic sacrifice we are most closely united to the working of the heavenly Church.'[93]

The fact that the Eucharist had an immediate effect on Christians in making them all feel they were one body, can be found in the Acts of the Apostles: 'Now the whole group of those who believed were of one heart and soul, and no one claimed private ownership of any possessions, but everything they owned was held in common.' (Acts. 4:32)

And John of Damascus writes: 'Communion too, is spoken of [referring to the Eucharist], and it is an actual communion, because through it we have communion with Christ, we have communion and are united with one another through it (we all become . . . members of one another, being of one body with Christ'.[94]

Origen, too, says that those who partake in the Eucharist must become conscious of the meaning of 'communion with the Church'. In fact, as one of Origen's commentators observes, 'communion with Christ's body is communion with his bread, but at the same time with his Church. The truth of the eucharistic assembly and of each of its participants is that their value is nothing less than that of the eucharistic bread itself'.[95]

Albert the Great emphasizes this reality in various passages: 'Just as bread, which is the matter of this sacrament, is made one from many grains which transmit their entire content to one another and penetrate one another, so too the true body of Christ is made up of many drops of blood of human nature . . . mixed with one another; and so also the many faithful, united in affection and communicating with Christ the head, mystically make up the one body of Christ . . . and thus this sacrament leads us to hold in common all our goods, both temporal and spiritual'.[96]

'In the elements of this sacrament communion is symbolized, which means the union of many in one, that is, in the bread and in the wine, because the bread is prepared from many grains and the wine from many grapes'.[97]

'By the very fact that [Christ] unites everyone to himself, he unites them to one another, because, if several things are united to a third, they are also united to one another'.[98]

Albert the Great again affirms that the true body of Christ is the cause of the unity of the mystical body, and that the special effect of the Eucharist is the grace of incorporation, which is the highest possible union.[99]

Pope Paul VI, Vicar of Christ, the Christ that we have been meditating upon as love, such great love, uses incomparable expressions to describe the Eucharist. I shall quote just one of them: 'the Eucharist . . . was instituted to make us brothers and sisters: . . . so that from being strangers who are scattered apart and indifferent towards one another, we become united, equals and friends. It is given to us so that from being an apathetic, egoistic mass, from people divided and hostile towards one another, we become a people, a true people, believing and loving, one heart and one soul'.[100]

The Eucharist and the Ideal of unity

Our Ideal is the Ideal of unity. Now, do you not think it is indicative that when Jesus spoke to his Father in that famous prayer, he asked for unity among his followers and among those who would come after him, after having instituted the Eucharist which made such a thing possible? Jesus, leaving the house on his way to the Garden of Olives, prayed: 'Holy Father, protect them in your name that you have given me, so that they may be one, as we are one'. (John 17: 11) We are united with another in the way that resembles the unity of the Father and the Son, thus we are completely one because of the Eucharist.

'I ask not only on behalf of these, but on behalf of those who will believe in me through their word, that they may all be one. As you, Father, are in me and I am in you, may they also be in us, so that the world will realize that it was you who sent me.' (John 17:21). We are in Jesus, who is in the Father, through the Eucharist.

'The glory that you have given me I have given them, so that they may be one, as we are one, I in them and you in me, that they may be completely one' (John 17:22-23).

We cannot enter the kingdom except in a unity with Jesus and with one another, by means of the Eucharist, like that of the Father and the Son who are one.

If we love our great Ideal, our vocation to unity, we must passionately love the Eucharist.

The Eucharist at Work in Us

The conditions for the full working of the Eucharist

We have seen the marvels the Eucharist accomplishes. It is logical that they occur in the believer when certain conditions are met.

Our incorporation into Christ, our personal deification, and our being completely one with the Church are at stake according to the attitude with which we receive communion.

According to the *Didache* and the early Fathers of the Church in general, and I shall soon quote from their works quite amply, the fundamental conditions are: to believe in Christ's doctrine; to be baptized; in particular to have faith in what the Eucharist is; to live according to Christ's teaching; to repent and confess one's sins so as to approach the Eucharist with a pure heart; to be reconciled with those brothers and sisters with whom one is not at peace; to be united to the Church, to the bishop; and to desire that union with Christ and with one's brothers and sisters which the Eucharist achieves.

In the *Didache* we read: 'You must not let anyone eat or

drink of your Eucharist except those baptized in the Lord's name. For in reference to this the Lord said, "Do not give what is sacred to dogs"'. (Matt. 7:6) On every Lord's Day - his special day come together and break bread and give thanks, first confessing your sins so that your sacrifice may be pure. Anyone at variance with his neighbour must not join you, until they are reconciled, lest your sacrifice be defiled.'[101]

'This food,' Justin affirms, 'we call Eucharist, of which no one is allowed to partake except one who believes that the things we teach are true, and has received the washing for the forgiveness of sins [baptism]'.[102]

'Let us approach the eucharistic mysteries,' says John Chrysostom, 'not only considering what falls beneath our senses, but holding fast to his words . . . Therefore, since the Word has said: "This is my body" [Matt. 26:26], let us submit and believe, looking upon this with the eyes of faith. In fact Christ did not give us anything sensible, but all spiritual realities although in sensible things . . . For if you were incorporeal he would have given you these incorporeal gifts without sensible signs, but since the soul is united to a body, he gives you spiritual realities in sensible things'.[103]

'Now,' and these are Origen's words, 'if anyone has to listen to the phrase, "Everyone should examine himself before eating this bread and drinking this cup" [1 Cor. 11:28], and neglects this warning, partaking of the bread and the chalice of the Lord in the state in which he finds himself, he becomes weak or sick, or even stunned (so to say) by the power of the bread, and dies.'[104]

Cyprian says: 'God does not accept the sacrifice offered by someone who nurtures enmity. He wants such a person to leave the altar and go first to reconcile himself with his brother, because God cannot be appeased by anyone who prays with his heart filled with hatred. The highest sacrifice in the eyes of God is our peace and brotherly concord, and his people gathered together in the unity of the Father, the Son and the Holy Spirit'.[105]

Again in John Chrysostom we find 'let nobody, therefore, be Judas . . . if you have some thing against your enemy, . . . put an end to your enmity, so that, from this table you may take the medicine [that is forgiveness] in fact, you are approaching a tremendous and holy sacrifice. Respect the meaning of this oblation. Christ lies sacrificed. For whom was he sacrificed and why? In order to reunite the things of above with those of below . . . to reconcile you with the God of the universe; to make you, who were once an enemy and adversary, a friend . . . He did not refuse to die for you, and you refuse to pardon your companion? . . . [This sacrifice] makes us all one body, since we all receive one Body. Therefore, let us unite ourselves in one Body . . . uniting our souls reciprocally with the bond of charity'.[106]

Finally, Ignatius of Antioch says: 'he who acts without the bishop's knowledge is in the devil's service'.[107]

The great theologians of the Middle Ages repeat the thought of the Fathers.

Albert the Great puts it like this: 'Because of this charity, which unites God with man and man with God [this sacrament] is called the sacrament of unity and of charity. Therefore we must eat this supper in the charity of ecclesial unity'.[108]

Thomas Aquinas says: 'This sacrament produces no effect in someone who is false. A person is false when his inner self does not correspond with what is signified externally. In the sacrament of the Eucharist what is externally signified is that Christ is incorporated with the person who receives him and the person is incorporated with Christ. Therefore, a person is false if there is no desire for this union in the heart and not even an attempt to remove every obstacle in the way of it. Therefore Christ does not remain in such persons nor they in Christ'.[109]

Pope Paul VI, as if summing up the spiritual dispositions that are necessary says: 'In the eucharistic kingdom whoever believes and loves, understands. Intelligence increases in proportion to love, to take possession of its object. In the conquest of divine things, love serves more than any other of our spiritual faculties.'[110]

If therefore, whoever draws near to the Eucharist wants to be in harmony with this sacrament, they must have firmly decided to carry out, with their will and in practice, what the Eucharist means and achieves: unity.

Other effects of the Eucharist

Now that we have considered the conditions necessary for the extraordinary graces which the Eucharist contains to take effect, let us see what else the Eucharist brings to our soul besides the principal effect of incorporating us with Christ and our brothers and sisters.

I mentioned that the Eucharist is also seen by the Church as the 'food for the journey' (in Latin *viaticum*) of the people of God on the way towards the goal. As such, it enriches the soul with an increase of love and a consequent diminution of the passions, as Thomas Aquinas says;[111] it brings comfort in sufferings and strength in struggles and trials, until we achieve sanctity and the everlasting life.

It is the Eucharist that gives 'divine charity', 'the light of wisdom', 'gladdens our hearts and souls' and 'warms man so much that it makes him come out of himself and reach the point of no longer seeing himself for himself, but himself for God, and God for God, and his neighbour for God', as Catherine of Siena says.[112]

For Paul of the Cross the Eucharist is, ' that angelic food which also contributes greatly to the strength of the body'.[113]

The Eucharist in the life of a Christian

Of course, eucharistic communion is not an end in itself. 'The union with Christ to which this sacrament is ordered must be continued throughout all Christian life. . . '[114]

There is the reality of the Church that gathers together for the eucharistic celebration, and witnesses the *ekklesia* (assembly), but there is also the reality of the Church that is spread throughout the world as the manifestation of Christ among human beings, as a sign of his presence.

The world does not receive the proclamation of Christ so much from the Eucharist as from the lives of Christians who are nourished on this Eucharist and on the Word, and who by preaching the Gospel with their lives and with their voices, make Christ present in the midst of humanity.[115]

United to Jesus Eucharist the Christian community can and must do what Jesus did: give its life for the world.

The life of the Church, thanks to the Eucharist, becomes the life of Jesus, and therefore a life capable of giving love, the life of God, to others, a life capable of saving, because it is the very life of Jesus which communicates itself to the community and to each individual member of it. In this sense we can understand Paul's words: 'I must go through the pain of giving birth to you all over again, until Christ is formed in you'. (Gal. 4:19)

Pope Paul VI says: '[The Lord] wanted to unite his divine life to ours so intimately, so lovingly, as to make himself our food, and thus to make us personally participants in his redemptive sacrifice . . . in order to involve us and to graft each one of us on to his plan of salvation, which is open to all humanity'.[116]

Emile Mersch explains: 'The act of Christ into which the Eucharist assimilates Christians is his sacrifice. Therefore, the Eucharist makes them a sacrifice, too, the Eucharist makes their life a sacrifice which continues the sacrifice of the head, and makes the cross take possession of mankind. The faithful, in him who makes total reparation for sin, will make reparation themselves, reparation in themselves and reparation throughout the whole Mystical Body, but a reparation which will be a continuation of Christ's, and will depend on and derive from Christ. It will be a reparation by members.

'This redeemer,' continues Emile Mersch, 'this Christ, in as much as he assimilates us to himself, is the Christ in the supreme act of his love, the Christ in that act in which, in a certain way, he "explodes" with love [in his abandonment, we would say] in order to be totally obedient to the Father and to be a complete offering to men. It is this explosion which penetrates Christians and transforms them into itself.

'We honour the Eucharist more through giving to our

neighbour than with beautiful ceremonies, even if the latter are necessary'.[117]

Besides, since modern theology has placed less emphasis on the presence of Jesus in the Eucharist, which the faithful are already well aware of, and more emphasis on spiritual union with him and with all the members of his Mystical Body, eucharistic spirituality too, is less directed nowadays towards adoring the Lord who is present and more towards communion with him and with our brothers and sisters, in every moment of the day.

The experience of the Focolare Movement

But let us pause for a second here.

As we read these texts about the conditions necessary for receiving the Eucharist and about the effects that it produces, did you not hear the Holy Spirit whispering in your heart, or better still, did you not almost feel like shouting out: 'But this is our Ideal! But this is our Ideal!'

I confess to you that when I read these things I was left astonished.

Do you remember, with what care right from the very first days we prepared ourselves in the morning for communion, making sure that the unity among us was perfect, and how we were ready to renounce receiving communion if this unity was lacking?

Do you remember how each morning we felt as if the Holy Spirit were knocking at our spirit's door and repeating tirelessly: 'if you remember that your brother or sister has something against you, leave your gift there before the altar and go; first be reconciled with your brother or sister'. (Cf. Matt. 4:23-24)

Do you remember the regular confessions, and the general confessions, which served to begin our new life better?

And that faith in the Church that did not tolerate any doubts? And how much, surpassing any other, our watchword was: 'Whoever listens to you, listens to me' (Luke 10:16), seeing in our bishop Christ to be obeyed?

Do you remember how deeply rooted the conviction was in us, as Cyprian says, that no penance and no sacrifice exceeded that of loving one another as Christ loved us?[118]

And it goes without saying, as Pope Paul VI affirms, that love was the strength in all our life.[119] And as to the effects, do you remember how, from the beginning, as our love grew, temptations that had been a torment for a lifetime disappeared as if by magic, only reappearing at times, months or years later, as trials sent by God, or if we slowed down our love.

And how much comfort Jesus in the Eucharist brought us in our trials, when nobody would receive us in audience because the Movement had to be studied. He was always there, at any hour, waiting for us, telling us: really I am the head of the Church.

And in the battles and sufferings of every kind, who gave us strength, so much so that we think we would have died many times if Jesus Eucharist and Jesus in our midst, whom he nourished, had not sustained us?

And that wisdom which the Movement has in such abundance, and the smile that characterizes its members, and our heart which so often bursts into flame, and our always living for God, and our saying and feeling that we are the most fortunate people in the world - where does all this come from?

Jesus Eucharist!

It is you who have made our whole life one continuous 'spiritual exercise', so that we never 'lose height', twenty four hours a day, and are always ready to climb up again if we stop.

And do you not remember how, from the very beginning, after meeting together at Mass, we would scatter out into the most varied places, from stables to schools and offices, and so on, to proclaim Christ, his new commandment, his Gospel, recounting not just the doctrine, but also the experience of our new life?

And the programme was not limited, it has always been 'May they all be one' - *Ut omnes* (John 17:21). We aimed at humanity, knowing that in order to save people, we, like Jesus, had first to pay with our lives and then speak.

It was obvious for us to offer our lives. Offering our lives whenever this was asked of us had always one aim: for the Church, for *Ut omnes* - 'May they all be one'.

This life has gone on for more than thirty years in our Movement, and as I meditated on the Eucharist in the last few days, I often asked myself: has the Eucharist been the moving force behind all our life?

Certainly there is a marvellous interwoven link between the Eucharist and the Ideal of unity. The fact that God, in order to begin this vast movement, concentrated our attention on the prayer of Jesus, on his last will and testament, means that he had to urge us forcefully towards the One who alone could achieve it: Jesus in the Eucharist.

Indeed, just as newborn babes nourish themselves instinctively at their mother's breast, without being aware of what they are doing, so too, from the beginning of the movement, we noted a phenomenon: those who met us began to go to daily communion.

How can we explain this? What instinct is for a newborn babe, the Holy Spirit is for an adult just born to the new life brought by the Gospel of unity. Such a person is driven towards the 'heart' of Mother Church and to be nourished on the most precious nectar she has. And the consequences follow.

Yes, it is our Ideal, the Ideal which we have always lived, in its essence, because our Ideal is nothing other than Christianity seen from unity, the Ideal of Christ.

The Eucharist and human social nature

I do not want to leave out a magnificent effect of the Eucharist that Pope Paul VI views as follows: '[This communion of supernatural life] can have an enormous and incomparably beneficial influence on the temporal social life of human beings. You know that the fundamental problem humanity's social life, which is at the forefront of all the other problems of our times, and dominates all of them, is how to create the earthly city; and we all know that those who try in many ways to accomplish this enormous feat are often able to make remarkable progress, but at every step they find in themselves obstacles and contradictions . . . precisely because they lack a single transcendent unifying principle for humanity's social life.

'The earthly city lacks that supplement of faith and love which it cannot find in itself and by itself, and which the religious city existing within the earthly one, that is the Church, can . . . through a silent osmosis of good example and spiritual virtue, abundantly bestow upon it'.[120]

'. . . therefore, is not the Eucharist a sign towards which the world, our modern world, must look with absolute sympathy if that unity which it seeks and produces, but then often breaks and fractures, yet always longs almost fatally for and rebuilds, if that unity is, let's say, the climax of the world's aspirations?'[121]

The Eucharist and the Holy Spirit

Now I would like to go on to say a few words about the Holy Spirit, in this conclusion to our brief talks on the Eucharist.

John, in his magnificent passage on the bread of life, quotes a saying of Jesus' that says: 'It is the Spirit that gives life; the flesh is useless'. (John 6:63)

In this saying Jesus refers to the Holy Spirit's role in the eucharistic mystery.

The Holy Spirit is the principal actor in every coming of Christ among us.[122]

It is through him that the Word became flesh in the womb of Mary, and it is through him that the Word becomes flesh in the host and blood in the wine during the eucharistic consecration.

Cyril of Jerusalem writes: 'Next, after sanctifying ourselves by those spiritual songs, we implore the merciful God to send forth his Holy Spirit upon the offering to make the bread the Body of Christ and the wine the Blood of Christ. For whatever the Holy Spirit touches is hallowed and changed.'[123]

As a result the Mass becomes a perpetuation of the incarnation. And this is magnificent, this is something to adore.

The theologian Betz writes that second century thinkers were of one mind with John in seeing 'in the eucharistic incarnation a sacramental continuation of Jesus' mission in the body'.[124]

Therefore the flesh on which we are nourished is a spiritualized flesh, the same flesh that Jesus has at the right hand of the Father. From this spiritualized flesh, which gives divine life, there is an outpouring of the Holy Spirit, who forms Christ within us because we have been fed by the Eucharist.

It is therefore the Holy Spirit who sanctifies us and so brings us to everlasting life.

It is through the Holy Spirit that Jesus rises in glory after his death.

It is he who descends to constitute the Church, the body of Christ.

It is also the Holy Spirit who brings about the unity of the community and sanctifies the community as such.

The Holy Spirit, the often silent God, as greatly active as he is little known, works continually as Love, who gives prominence to the Father and the Son.

The plan of God for the total Christ is, as I have already mentioned, a magnificent journey: from the Trinity to the Trinity.

The Father loves us and sends the Son, but among the things that the Son has to carry out, in agreement with the Father, there is the Eucharist. If the Son is one of the Father's gifts to us, the Eucharist is a gift of the One who is given. When a person who is well-disposed receives the

Eucharist, he or she is incorporated with the Son and with his brothers and sisters, and returns to the bosom of the Father.

The Second Vatican Council describes this: 'In this mystery the faithful united with their bishops, have access to God the Father, through the Son, in the outpouring of the Holy Spirit . . . they enter into communion with the most Holy Trinity.'[125]

We know of saints and others who have been given some task by God in the Church to whom he has revealed, in greater or lesser depth, this immanence in the Father's bosom.

Usually for everybody this is not so. Instead it is rather a being in the Father's bosom and a perennial nostalgia to get there.

The Eucharist, in fact, is food that gives life, food that strengthens and fortifies in an even greater way, and we must eat this food often in order to be able to say: 'it is no longer I who live, but it is Christ who lives in me.' (Gal. 2:20)

Jesus, when I was preparing to say something about you in the Eucharist, I think my heart almost burned in my breast. I at once perceived what I was about to do: to say something about you in four poor talks. And my desire would have driven me to build you a cathedral.

Now I realize that perhaps the result is a poor wooden altar. I am not capable of talking about you: you are too great.

One day I read that if the Church did not have the Eucharist it would not have the strength to raise itself up towards God, and for this reason the Eucharist is considered to be the heart of the Church. Pardon my temerity, therefore.

But, since your game is to draw great things from weakness, here are these pages as a gift of love to your measureless love. Use them so that others may be able to understand you a bit more, and, with your strength, unleash the Christian revolution in the world.

Where Two or Three

Jesus in our Midst

In our life we have without a doubt given the foremost place to 'Jesus in our midst'. In fact, we know that everything we do is of value if Jesus is in our midst, and nothing is of value if Jesus is not in our midst.

As we wrote in our statutes, he is 'the norm of norms, the rule that precedes every other rule' for each member of the Focolare Movement. But as I prepare to speak to you about Jesus in our midst, I feel how arid and cold juridical expressions are. Jesus in the midst is not just a norm or a rule, even though it is true that he is the premise for every rule. Jesus in the midst is a person! The most holy and glorious person, Jesus; and we shall be speaking about him today and in the days to come.

When the Focolare Movement first began, in the Roman Catholic world there was not much talk about Jesus in the midst of people. The words of Jesus: 'where two or three are gathered together in my name, I am there among them,' which we find in Matthew's Gospel, chapter 18, verse 20, were not particularly emphasized.

Even people in authority, our superiors, however much they loved us, one day directed us not to talk about Jesus in the midst. But they retracted these instructions immediately afterwards, and we think it was the Holy Spirit who made them do so, leaving us completely free to emphasize these words of Jesus.

For us, from the very beginning, Jesus in the midst was everything: he was life.

Now that the Second Vatican Council has spoken about Jesus in the midst in such an explicit way, it has become something normal for many people.

But for my own and for all of our consolation, I wanted to see if in the early Church this sentence of the Gospel was given the importance we give, owing, I think, to the presence of a charism.

When reading the Fathers of the Church, for example, I was astonished to see their line of thought in this regard, and through my contact with them, whom I can consider my Fathers, Jesus in the midst took on an even greater universality than I had first been aware of in my soul.

Indeed, to explain the presence of God within the Church, which is of the greatest importance, since the Church without Christ in it would be nothing, the Fathers base their explanation on two sentences: 'Where two or three are gathered together in my name, I am there among them' and 'I am with you always, to the end of the age.' (Matt. 28:20) Therefore, we are not talking about a minor activity to which some people out of habit may have reduced life with Jesus in the midst, when they come together with others in this way. No, living with Jesus in the midst makes us much more vitally a part of the presence of Jesus in his Church. Anyone who is sensitive to the things of God and lives this way, cannot help but feel privileged among all the people of this world.

Jesus in the midst is God among us

We all know that the major choice of the Movement and of each one of us was God. Against the vanity of all things, God shone out as a certainty. We adored him present in tabernacles, we loved him in our brothers and sisters, we contemplated him beyond the stars in the immensity of the universe. But God who was so present with his love, yet so distant with his majesty, had come close to us, had come among us met together, and made there his dwelling place.

Origen says: 'with his power he [the Son of God] is near everyone . . . In fact, he himself said: "I am a God who is near." [Cf. Jer. 23:23] And he himself also said: "Where two or three are gathered together in my name, there am I in the midst of them."'[126]

It is magnificent. And we have had this good fortune.

Origen identifies Jesus in the midst with the 'God who is near' as emphasized in the Old Testament.

Eusebius of Caesarea, in his commentary on the book of Zechariah, writes: '"Sing and rejoice (O Church), daughter of Zion (Scripture often calls the Church of God on earth the daughter of the Church which is in heaven)! For lo, I will come and I dwell in your midst" [Zech. 2:10] . . . In fact we believe, that God, the Word, lives in the Church, as he himself promised when he said: and 'And remember, I am with you always, to the end of the age' [Matt. 28: 20] and "where two or three are gathered together in my name, I am there among them".'[127]

Eusebius also wrote: 'O Lord, I love and prefer your dwelling place, because you yourself have deigned to live here among us and to set here your residence; in fact, you said:

"where two or three are gathered together in my name, I am there among them."'[128]

John Chrysostom wrote: 'greater than their dignity as seraphim is the fact that they stand around the throne [of God] and that he is in their midst. But, if you wish, you can obtain this privilege, too: in fact, God is not just in the midst of the seraphim but is also in our midst, if we want this. "Because," it is written, "where two or three are gathered together in my name, there am I in the midst of them".'[129]

Jesus in the midst is one of his presences

Without doing a lot of theological or philosophical reasoning, throughout the life of the Movement we have always understood that the presence of Jesus is not limited to his physical presence, that was once on earth, in the past, and is now in heaven. There is the presence of Jesus in our midst, Jesus in the Eucharist, Jesus in his word, Jesus in our neighbour, Jesus in the hierarchy.

Origen, the Father of the Church who commented the most on Matthew 18:20, says: 'The Gospels consider that he [the Word of God] who in the person of Jesus says these words: "I am the way, and the truth and the life," [John. 14:6] this Word of God is not limited to the point of not existing in any way outside the body and soul of Jesus . . . Jesus himself raises his disciples' intelligence to higher concepts of the Son of God when he says: "Where two or three are gathered together in my name, there am I in the midst of them."'[130]

Origen also says: 'do not be afraid of anything because Jesus Christ though he is now assumed into heaven, will come again . . . I repeat, do not be afraid, because Jesus Christ comes now, too . . . It is not a lie. "Where two or three are gathered together in my name, there am I in the midst of them."'[131]

Cyril of Alexandria says: 'all those who think rightly and have a firm faith must be convinced that, though he is far from us with his body, that is, though he has returned to God, to the Father, nonetheless he governs the world with his divine power and authority and he is present in the midst of those who love him. Thus he said, "Truly, truly I say to you, where two or three are gathered together in my name, there am I in the midst of them."'[132]

Jesus in the midst is immediately present

We establish the presence of Jesus in the midst when we want it. We can live it immediately. Origen says that 'one should pay close attention to the words of the Lord, because he did not say: "Where two or three . . . there I shall be in the midst of them" but "there I am" [in the midst of them]'.[133]

As Theofilatus, Bishop of Bulgaria, says: 'He does not say "I shall be" in fact, he does not delay or hesitate – but "I am" that is, "I am already there"'.[134]

Jesus in the midst is the Church

We have always liked Tertullian's saying: 'Where three are gathered together even if they are lay people, there is the Church.'[135]

Yes, because we are often a small group united and bound

juridically with the entire Church of Christ. Therefore, even if there are only a few of us, we are 'Church', 'living Church', through the presence of Jesus among us.

We find this confirmed by John of Ciparissia: 'what is the Church of God? . . . it is the sacred meeting in the name of the true light that enlightens everyone who comes into the world, a meeting which arises and grows not only from multitudes of distinguished people, but also from those who are humble. In fact, there is a passage where the Word of God said: "Where two or three are gathered together in my name, there am I in the midst of them."'[136]

Jesus in the midst generates the churches

Since we are 'Church', we are capable of giving life to the churches. This is what happens with missionaries who go to some distant place that has not yet been evangelized and who found a Church, the local Church.

This is what happened with us, too, in Fontem (Cameroon) for example, where the first two or three focolarini, though they were laymen, succeeded in building up a parish which is an integral part of the diocese of Buea, because Christ was among them.

Eusebius of Caesarea used the name 'city of God' for the universal Church and 'houses of this city' for the local Christian communities, to which he often applies Matthew 18:20. He says: 'The Churches, established all over the world, are those houses in whose midst God is always present, God who said, "Where two or three are gathered together [in my name] there am I in the midst of them."'[137]

And elsewhere, Eusebius also affirms: 'These idolatrous forms ended when Churches were founded in all of Egypt and the Lord himself went there and visited his Churches in accordance with what he had said: "Where two or three are gathered together in my name, there am I in the midst of them."'[138]

Jesus in the midst means salvation in difficult situations

Jesus in the midst is the salvation of the Movement and is the possibility of its life in places where external conditions hinder its freedom to develop, either because of other religions intolerant towards ours, or because of an environment that has become dechristianized by a materialistic mentality and way of life, or because of the absence of any knowledge of Jesus, as in non-evangelized countries. In these places our homes are our meeting places and Jesus in the midst makes them churches.

Circumstances of this kind take us back to the situation of the primitive Church.

In the *Apostolic Constitutions*, which is the most important collection of juridical and liturgical statements of early Christian times, we find the following conclusion: 'If because of non-believers, it is impossible for you to meet together in a home or in a church, let each of you sing psalms, read [scripture] and pray in his own home, especially two or three of you together, because "where two or three are gathered together in my name, there am I in the midst of them."'[139]

And Tertullian in *De fuga in persecutione* writes: 'Are you unable to go to every meeting ? For you, even if there are only three of you, there is the Church.'[140]

And Theodore of Studium advises: 'Brothers and Fathers, God has granted us a supreme favour, that of being persecuted for his sake, as the Gospel says: "Blessed are they who suffer persecution for the sake of righteousness, for theirs is the kingdom of heaven." [Matt. 5:10]

'But we must take care that it is not because we live a life unworthy of beatitude, a life not according to the Gospel, that we receive persecution as a punishment.

'Therefore, someone who is persecuted must, first of all, not live alone, but live together with another brother, because "Where two or three are gathered together in my name, there am I in the midst of them," says the Lord.'[141]

For Theodore, Jesus in the midst guarantees the genuineness of a life lived according to the Gospel.

Jesus in the midst unites us even at a distance

Athanasius applies Matthew 18:20 also to those who are far away from one another but are spiritually united. This is a great joy for us: 'although distance divides us, nonetheless . . . the Lord . . . unites us spiritually in harmony and the bond of peace.

'When we have these sentiments and raise the same prayers [to God], no distance can separate us because the Lord unites us and binds us closely together. In fact, where two or three are gathered together in his name, he himself is present in the midst of them, as he promised.'[142]

Jesus in the midst means unity with the whole Church

There is a mysterious and marvellous fact in our life in the Ideal.[143] Who was it who always convinced us, beyond the slightest doubt, that everything we did was of value if it was done in unity with the Church, which is constructed hierarchically? Who was it who impressed in our hearts that the Church has always been a mother to us, and that as a consequence our lives had to be lived as children of this mother, even when someone not too well-versed in the works of God might have doubted it? Who was it that gave value to Jesus in the midst whom we tried to have present in all our meetings, if not the faith and conviction that he was there in our midst because our little group was united to the whole of the Church and to all its pastors?

Thinking back on it now, thinking of how young we were at that time, it is enough to make us pause for a moment. We could have erred a thousand times on this point, but we never did. The conclusion is that he who guided us in this way was the Holy Spirit.

On this point, too, the Fathers forcefully confirm our line of action.

Cyprian says: 'And let no one be deceived with an interpretation that empties these words of their meaning, the words of the Lord: "Where two or three are gathered together in my name, there I shall be with them." He [Jesus] teaches us that we must be always closely united together.

'Now, how is it possible for one be in agreement with another if not in agreement with the whole body of the Church and with the entire community of the brothers and sisters? How can two or three be gathered in the name of

Christ, when it is known that they are separated from Christ and from his Gospel? For we did not separate from them, they were the ones who abandoned the source and the origin of the truth, forming conventicles for themselves.

'But the Lord is speaking of his Church, to those who are in the Church: if they are in agreement, since he commanded and admonished that two or three pray united together, but united unanimously, then they shall obtain from God's majesty whatever they ask . . .

'Therefore, when among his precepts he says: "Where there are two or three, I shall be with them," he who instituted and formed the Church does not divide people from the Church'.[144]

Jesus in our midst, a brother among his brothers and sisters, master, guide, comfort, light: we have no reason to envy those who lived near him in Palestine. We have everything to hope for from his ultra-extraordinary promise. He is the source of a divine fire in the world, wherever he is present, he who said: 'I came to bring fire upon the earth.' (Luke 12:49)

We have an immense treasure, we have the treasure; let's leave everything in order to possess it. He will give us Paradise on earth and Paradise in the next life.

Being Alone and Being United

Let's say something now about being alone and being united.

I remember that especially in the beginning when we first started to live this spirit, each one of us felt very strongly the difference between being united and being alone without the help of unity.

When we were alone, detached from the community, we became aware of all our personal fragility, we felt we were very lost and that our will was weak and indecisive. We could not see why we had left everything to follow Jesus; the light was missing, yes, the Light. Regarding this I remember one day I was alone in the first focolare, preparing lunch. Through some one's lack of virtue, before each of us had left for work, we had said goodbye but not in full unity. I could not understand anything anymore. I could not see the reason for the many sacrifices I had made to follow Jesus, like having left my relatives whom I loved so much; I could not see the reason why I had abandoned so many things for him, like my studies, for example. I found myself at one moment up in the attic getting wood for the fire and I caught sight of the boxes of my beloved books. . . I remember the tears that fell on to the dust which had covered that previous love of mine. And I decided to wait for my friends in order to put Jesus back in our midst in order to see again. And that is what happened.

In being united, on the other hand, we felt the strength of Jesus among us. It was as if we were all clothed in the power and blessing of heaven. We felt capable of the noblest actions for God, of the most ardent and difficult resolutions that we then carried out, whereas before, when we were alone, no matter how much good will we might have had, it was difficult to live up fully to the promises we had made to the Lord. We felt a power that was not human.

One of the things that young people have to overcome, for example, is human respect. In unity, this problem no longer existed, not through anyone's personal virtue, but through the strength of unity. We spoke instead of 'divine respect', that is, our duty of respecting and witnessing to the things of God.

If before this new life began we had been convinced that it was impossible to live the Gospel in our times, because by ourselves we had not succeeded in doing it, in unity we saw that it was possible. This was an immense discovery that was very rich in consequences, and it was the cause of the birth of such a vast Movement.

The Fathers of the Church use magnificent words in praise of being together and they warn against solitude.

Gregory of Agrigentus says: 'Besides, even if we find that a man on his own, whom we know is good and humane, is better than another who has no humanity ... nonetheless wise Ecclesiastes takes honest and unanimous men two by two, and eliminates from the outset any possible objection to this idea by saying, "If they fall, one will lift up his companion". [Cf. Eccles. 4:10]

'In fact, if someone has fallen into what is unlawful and does not find another person anywhere to lift him up and call him back to a better life, it is clear that his fall and his sinful aberration will remain and nothing will be changed or corrected.

'Therefore, our Lord says in the Gospel: "Where two or three are gathered together in my name, there am I in the midst of them", thus clearly teaching us that harmonious agreement and union between two or three in what is good is much more important than [the goodness] of only one'.[145]

And Niceta Pectoratus writes: 'To meet together in a single home is safer than being alone. The holy word of our Lord Jesus, in fact, witnesses to the necessity of meeting together, because: "Where two or three are gathered together in my name, there am I in the midst of them."' Concerning the danger of solitude, Solomon says: "Woe to the one who is alone, when he falls and has not another to lift him up." [Eccles. 4: 10b] . . . And regarding the disciples of the Lord it is said: "They were of one heart and soul." [Acts 4:32]

'It is therefore necessary that we live together in harmony, whereas solitude is insecure and dangerous.'[146]

In his commentary on Psalm 133, 'How good and pleasant it is when kindred live together in unity! . . . For there the Lord ordained his blessing,' John Chrysostom explains: 'There: but where? Wherever there is such a dwelling place, such harmony, such accord, such a way of living together. Because in this there is a blessing, just as in its opposite there is a curse.

'For this reason it is praised, and it can indeed be said "a brother helped by another brother is like a fortified city"'. (Cf. Prov. 18:19)[147]

In yet another place John Chrysostom splendidly affirms:

'Great is the strength that comes from meeting together . . . because, when we are gathered together, charity grows, and if charity grows, the reality of God necessarily grows [among us].'[148]

He gives as an example the unity between Peter and John, in his commentary on the verse from the Acts of the Apostles: 'One day Peter and John were going up to the temple at the hour of prayer, at three o'clock in the afternoon.' (Acts 3:1) He writes: 'Do not overlook this account through negligence, but stop at once at the introduction, and try to learn how great their charity was, how great their harmony and accord, and how they communicated everything to one another and did all things bound by the tie of friendship in God, and how they appeared together when at table, at prayer, when walking and in every other action. Because, if they who were the pillars and the towers [of the Church] and who enjoyed great trust from God needed mutual help and corrected one another, how much more in need of mutual help are we, who weak, wretched, worthless?

'Thus were Peter and John', continues Chrysostom, 'and they had Jesus in the midst (*habebant Jesum in medio*). "Where two or three are gathered together in my name," He says in fact, "there am I in the midst of them."

'Do you understand how important it is to be united?'[149]

The conditions for having Jesus in the midst

But what are the conditions for having Jesus in the midst?

We know the answer: we have Jesus in our midst if we are united in his name. This means if we are united in him, in his will, in love which is his will, in mutual love which is the supreme will of Jesus, his commandment; where there is unity of sentiment, of will, and of thought, if possible in all things, but decisively in our faith.

The Fathers of the Church also ask themselves what conditions are required for having Jesus in the midst and from their texts we can realize that while one sees things from one point of view, another sees them from another.

Basil asks himself: 'In what way can we become worthy of having Jesus among us gathered together in his name?' And he states that to live according to the will of God is the essential condition.

He says: 'Those who meet together in the name of somebody must know well the will of the person who has gathered them together and must conform themselves to that will . . .

'And so we [monks] who have been called by the Lord, have to remember what the Apostle [Paul] said: "I . . . beg you to lead a life worthy of the calling to which you have been called . . . making every effort to maintain the unity of the Spirit in the bond of peace. There is one body and one Spirit . . ." [Eph. 4:1-4]'[150]

For Basil, therefore, to do the will of God is the condition for having Jesus in the midst.

John Chrysostom makes the condition for having Jesus in the midst, love for our brother or sister for love of Jesus, a love that is like the love of Jesus who gave his life for his enemies.

He explains the saying: 'Where two or three are gathered together in my name, I am there among them' by saying: 'What then? Cannot we find two or three gathered together in his name ? Yes, but rarely so. In fact Jesus does not merely speak of meeting physically . . . His words have this meaning:

if anyone has me as the principal cause of his love towards his neighbour, then I will be with him . . . Nowadays, instead, we see that the great majority of people have other motives for their friendship. One loves because of being loved, another loves because of being honoured, a third loves because someone has been useful in some worldly affair; another loves for other similar reasons. But it's difficult to find somebody who loves his or her neighbour for Christ, as we must love . . . Those who love in this manner [that is, for Christ], even if they are hated, insulted, or threatened with death, go on loving . . . Because in this way Christ loved his enemies . . . with the greatest love'[151]

For Chrysostom, therefore, to love the way that Jesus loved, is the condition for having Jesus in the midst.

Theodore of Studium finds in mutual love the condition for having Jesus in the midst of us. He writes:

'Therefore I heartily beg you in the Lord, not just to look after your own security but to take care of your brothers and sisters, too, so that you may be loved by them and in your turn love them, in this way you will be loved and you will love.

'In fact, where there is spiritual charity, there Christ is in the midst, as he promised.'[152]

Origen holds that the condition for having Jesus in the midst is agreement between several people in thought and in sentiment so as to reach, as he says magnificently, 'that concord which unites and which contains the Son of God.'[153]

Origen also affirms: 'wherever Christ sees two or three gathered together in faith in his name, he goes there and is in the midst of them, drawn by their faith and attracted by their unanimity.'[154]

In his view, it is always only a few who are united in such

a way as to have Christ present, and among the examples he gives are Peter, James and John, to whom, 'since they were in agreement, the word of God revealed his Glory', and Paul and Sosthenes who 'agreed with one another when they sent the first letter to the Corinthians.' And 'likewise Paul and Timothy when they wrote the second letter to the same community. In fact, there were three in agreement when Paul, Silvanus and Timothy wrote a letter of instruction to the Thessalonians.'[155]

But he also mentions the first Christians who were 'one heart and one soul', adding, however, 'if it is possible for this to happen among many people'.[156]

What stands out, following these thoughts, is the great value of the vocation of our Movement. In it a life is extended to many, which some Fathers of the Church maintained belonged only to a few, while others saw it as the vocation of the entire Church. Let us, therefore, be grateful to God and commit ourselves with all our souls to this vocation which we see is still so rare in the world today.

The value of Jesus in the midst

But what is the value of Jesus in the midst?

In the first years of the Movement, when the enthusiasm of 'beginners' prevailed, in a warm, filial conversation which I had with the then Monsignor Montini, we spoke about the way we Christians often invert values when we consider the various riches of the Church. Our brief conversation concerned, in fact, the value of Jesus in the midst, and the ideas it contained were more or less as follows:

'If we are united, Jesus is among us. And this has value. It is worth more than our heart may possess; more than mother, father, brothers, sisters, children. It is worth more than our house, our work, or our property; more than the works of art in great city like Rome; more than our business deals; more than nature which surrounds us with flowers and fields, the sea and stars; more than our own soul!'

I was particularly happy to find recently, a commentary in Gregory Nazianzen, that is in harmony with that conversation. In his famous farewell address to Constantinople, in the presence of bishops and the public, he says: 'But you [Constantinople] ardently loved frescoes, paintings, tombstones carved with art and elegance, along arcades and galleries, and you shone all ablaze with gold . . . certainly not knowing that . . . three who are gathered together in the name of the Lord are deemed by God more numerous than many thousands who deny his divinity' (that is, more than your entire population).[157]

I also recall, regarding the value of Jesus in the midst, the brief words which Pasquale Foresi addressed to the small group of focolarini present at the farewell Mass at the close of his first visit to the USA. He said that he had seen many very beautiful things in New York City, but that the most beautiful of all for him was that tiny group of focolarini who had Jesus in their midst.

Jesus in the midst illuminates

Jesus in the midst illuminates.

Pope Paul VI in his homily to twenty-five thousand young

people in St Peter's who had come for the Holy Year, on the day following the Genfest[158] held in the Sport's Stadium, Rome, invited us to follow two sayings from the Gospel, one of which was: 'You have only one Teacher.' (Cf. Matt. 23, 8-10).[159] With this he stressed what has been our line of action right from the beginning.

Who enlightened us about the sayings of the Gospel, so that we saw it as something completely new, revolutionary, and full of life? Jesus in our midst.

Origen says that Jesus, present among people who are united in his name, 'is willing to illuminate the hearts of those who want to understand his doctrine.'[160] With these words he leads us to understand that it is a vital and wise illumination that extends to the whole person, and not just an intellectual illumination.

And who, then, throughout the entire history of the Movement, drew lines of light for the organization of the Movement? Who gave birth to the various vocations, if not he? Each vocation is divine and so, too, is every application of the same Ideal to the various vocations. He is behind our rules of life; he is behind every step we take.

And when we do not know how to act, who else do we turn to but him, saying to each other: 'Come, let's put Jesus in the midst in order to understand the will of God?' He alone is the light of our life, the solution of all our problems.

Origen realized this, too, when he wrote: 'If we are not able to solve or explain some problem, let us draw near to Jesus in full agreement of feelings about our request, because he is present where two or three have met in his name, and while he is present with his might and power, he is willing to illuminate hearts . . . so that we may penetrate the questions with our soul.'[161]

Jesus in the midst is celebration

When Jesus is in our midst it is always a celebration. If there is one thing characteristic of our meetings, both small and large, it is the fullness of joy that emanates from each person and lights up their face. And often when you take part in one of these meetings you find yourself thinking that perhaps it is a holiday. Alternatively it happens that some Sunday when you find yourself all alone without the company of your brothers or sisters, the day loses the splendour of the Lord's day.

Yes, because Jesus in the midst of a few people or many people who have met together in his name is the Jesus of celebration, Jesus of the resurrection, who now, besides living at the right hand of the Father, also lives in the little churches made up of several Christians.

John Chrysostom says: 'Even though Pentecost day is over, the feast is not at an end; in fact, each meeting is a celebration. What is the cause of this? The very words of Christ who says: 'Wherever two or three are gathered together in my name, there am I in the midst of them.' Therefore, each time that Christ is present in the midst of a meeting, what greater proof do you want for it being a celebration.'[162]

When Jesus is in our midst it is a celebration for us and also for him.

Theofilatus confirms this: 'Truly God rejoices not because of a great crowd, but rather "where two or three are gathered together in his name, there he is in the midst of them."'[163]

If God rejoices where there is unity, what ideal could be greater than to make our life a succession of days that add additional joy to the happiness that Jesus already experiences?

His love for us, his daily, immeasurable love, that comes to us in big and small things deserves and demands this response.

Jesus in the Midst in the Life of the Community

Christianity in its various manifestations, as we know, is always new and always the same.

If we wanted to say what a focolare[164] is in a few words we can and must define it as being a small community which has Jesus in its midst.

When God thought of founding monasteries, for example, his idea was the very same.

Besides, what other idea could God have after having sent his Son for the salvation of the human race if not the idea of in some way giving life to his presence among people in order to continue his presence?

We find in the writings of Theodore Balsamon: 'Therefore we say that since the mouth of God has declared, "where two or three are gathered together in my name, there am I in the midst of them," it is necessary that there should be at least three to found anything that goes by the name of monastery.'[165]

A monastery, therefore, is a real monastery if it has the presence of Jesus among at least three members.

Of course, although Christianity is always the same, and

this praises God's unity, there are no two cases completely alike, just as no tree has two leaves that are exactly the same, and this praises the trinity of God.

A focolare is one thing and a monastery is another. The focolare with Jesus in the midst has norms that we believe to be inspired, and they are sacred and have been approved by the Church.

The focolare is a house in which life is ordered according to precise aspects that we all know, which range from the complete communion of goods to a specific apostolate, to set prayers, to levels of formation for its members who have left the world for God consecrating themselves with vows, to a particular way of considering physical health, to a particular way of laying out the various areas of the house, to studies, both religious and secular, and the unity of all the members spread all over the world, which is maintained with all available means. These aspects embody and in their turn facilitate the presence of Jesus in our midst.

On the other hand, what is the definition of a monastery?

John, Bishop of Antioch, tells us: 'Do you not know what a monastery is? It is a house that is wholly sacred, built in the name of Christ our God, and in its holy, innermost rooms there are paintings of him and of his miracles and divine sufferings. In the temple there are sacred books and the precious vestments and vessels.

'There is the holy community of those who for God have renounced the world, everything in the world, and their very selves. They stay close to God, they listen to him day and night, they sing and recite psalms . . . and they always have him in their midst, according to his most certain and divine promise, "where two or three are gathered together in my name," he said, "there I am in their midst." '[166]

Basil in his rule for the Eastern monks, identifies monastic life with being gathered together in the name of Jesus.

The value that he gives to a life in common probably came from his personal experience. In fact, Gregory the Presbyter, wrote that Basil and Gregory Nazianzen, 'instructed together in literary studies and separated from one another for a short period of time, hurried again to be near one another . . . so that in them these words were fulfilled: "Where two or three are gathered together in my name, there am I in the midst of them". Moreover, remaining here together, they grew in virtue, mutually stimulating one another, and drew up the laws of monastic life for religious men who are consecrated to God and detached from the world.'[167]

As I begin to deepen my knowledge of the presence of Jesus in our midst, I understand more and more its immense wealth and divine reality. When two of us are united in focolare, we are not two, let's remind ourselves, we are three. When we are three, we are four - we must open the eyes of our souls to see Jesus always there with us, taking part in our study, our work, our sufferings and our joys.

We must be careful to welcome in our life all the value and all the effects that this presence involves.

At times, for example, we might be led to make the presence of Jesus in the midst a mere instrument for the apostolate of the focolare, since we know how extraordinarily effective it is, and we could live without seeing the focolare as a jewel in itself and for itself. What Basil says seems applicable to us: 'We must carry out every action in a manner befitting an action performed in the sight of God who is present, and think every thought in a manner befitting a thought which he who is present scrutinizes.'[168]

The focolarini have certain devotions and prayers established by their statute which they perform individually, owing to the type of life that characterizes the focolare, wherever the will of God places them. Only in the Centres of the Movement are we invited to carry out these prayers and devotions together.

Here, too, Basil can be found helpful by focolarini in this thought of his: 'If by chance there are some [monks] who because of their work or because of the distance between places are not able to be present because they are too far away, then without any hesitation, wherever they are, they must necessarily perform each single prayer that has already been established in common, because "if two or three are gathered together in my name," says the Lord "I am there in the midst of them."'[169]

Therefore when we pray we must realize we are united to the chorus of prayers that all the focolarini of the world send up to God and be convinced, as Basil also says, that: 'Prayer itself that does not come from persons praying together is much feebler, since the Lord has declared that he will be in the midst if two or three who call upon him in communion of spirit.'[170]

Basil mentions Jesus in the midst again in various points of his rule. One part which I feel is particularly interesting for us is this magnificent passage, which regards poverty and God's providence.

The focolarini, too, have placed all their goods in common, 'down to the last pin' as we say, and they, too, are daily witnesses of the providence of God, which is usually never lacking if we live the spirit of Christ. This phenomenon amazes us and shows us the truth of Jesus' promise that he would give the hundredfold in brothers, sisters, mothers, and goods to those who would follow him and leave every thing. (Cf. Matt. 19:29; Mark 10:30)

Basil, therefore, says: 'Once an ascetic has taken up the life in common which we have spoken about, it is fitting that he should be free of all private possession of earthly goods. Because if he is not free in this way, in the first place with his private property he ruins a perfect and pure communion, and in the second place he reveals himself to be very unbelieving, as though he were not confident that God would nourish those who are gathered together in his name.

'In fact, if where two or three are gathered together in the name of Christ, he is there in the midst of them, then there is all the more reason for him to be where there is a meeting of a much larger number of people who are much more assiduous in their meeting.

'Therefore, either we will not lack anything necessary provided that Christ is present among us, just as the Israelites in the desert lacked nothing that was useful to them; or else, even if we are lacking in something in order to test us, it is better for us to be in need and be with Christ rather than to possess all the wealth of the world out of union with him.'[171]

What we have said here about the focolare certainly also applies to those other forms of life of unity present in the Movement which could be called temporary focolares, such as the nuclei of volunteers, of priests, of religious, men and women, the Gen units and so on, provided that all day long they stay in unity of spirit with the other members of the nucleus or unit, and with the whole Work of Mary, so as always to have the presence of Jesus in the midst.

And what we have said here about the focolare also applies to those larger forms of community life, where at the same time there are focolares, nuclei, units, new families, and new religious communities..., that is to say, our little towns that reproduce today in modern form those communities which once arose around Benedictine monasteries and abbeys and which were real little towns.

While allowing for inevitable human limitations, I think we can wish for our little towns what Theodore of Studium wished when he wrote to a monastery that had Jesus in the midst: 'What else, therefore, is left to say? That, just as the grace of our Lord Jesus Christ has brought you together and bound you in spiritual accord, and you are renowned for your unanimous concord and you shine out in these places like certain stars in the dark night of heresy, remain like this in the future, as you are, unanimous, with the same sentiments, the same thoughts ... luminous and bright and radiant, and also full of wisdom, so that the Lord may say deservedly of you, "You are the light of the world" [Matt. 5:14a], and also "You are the salt of the earth" [Matt. 5:13a]. And perhaps, also, because you live in mountainous places, may it fittingly be sung of you: "A city set on a mountain cannot be hidden," [Matt. 5:14b] – certainly it is the mountain of sublime life in common and those who have climbed it live there on earth as it is in heaven [cf. Matt. 6:10]; the world is not worthy of them, as the Apostle has said [cf. Heb. 11:38].'[172]

Consenserint

There is a prayer which the members of the Movement have used for thirty years, ever since the Movement began. If they are asked to pray in any kind of circumstance, for the living or for the dead, or to obtain any grace at all, they make a consenserint, i.e., united in the name of Jesus, they ask the Eternal Father anything whatsoever. The Latin word consenserint is taken from Jesus' phrase: 'Again I tell you, if two of you agree (*consenserint*) on earth about anything you ask, it will be done for you by my Father in heaven. For where two or three are gathered together in my name, I am there among them.' (Matt. 18:19-20)

Certainly we do not neglect the other prayers that the Church recommends, but this prayer, I would say, is our prayer. In this prayer we know that it is not we who ask, but Jesus who is present in our unity. And through this prayer countless spiritual and material graces have been showered on the Movement.

John Chrysostom says that no one meets together with others to pray 'trusting in his or her own virtue, but rather in the community and in the accord which God holds in the highest consideration and by which he is moved and appeased.

'"Since, where two or three are gathered together in my name," he said, "there am I in the midst of them" . . . In fact, what a person cannot obtain praying alone, can be obtained by praying together with the community. Why ? Because even if a person's own virtue has not great power, unanimity has great power "where two or three are gathered together."'[173]

Another aspect of the consenserint which has always been

present in the Movement as a light of hope in a truly evangelical dimension, is that 'anything' which Jesus says we are to ask for. 'Anything': therefore everything, from little things to big ones, from things of the body to things of the spirit. Everything can be requested in unity. And everything is requested in unity.

Peter Chrysologus, in one of his sermons, confirms that when the Lord says, '"if . . . they agree to ask anything, it will be granted them," he does not promise to grant one thing or another, but everything that is asked for with a unanimous request.'[174]

In our Movement, we have not neglected individual prayer. The way of sanctity upon which our spirituality sets us, developing its various stages, also deepens our personal union with God, which brings us to ask the Lord for many things.

But we are in full agreement with what Peter Chrysologus also says: 'How can you despise the assembly of the Church and assert that the prayers of individuals should be placed before those of the venerable assembly, if the Lord promises to be present in the midst of two or three gathered together and to grant them everything they request of him?'[175]

Therefore it is not individualism that pleases God but unity.

Of course, we have always held that the above mentioned sentence of the Gospel obtains its end if it is lived together with all the rest of the Gospel. For this reason before making a consenserint we examine ourselves to see if we are ready to die for one another, and we do not diminish this readiness after having prayed. For us the consenserint is the prayer of someone who lives the Gospel, and not a magic formula for those who need to obtain something.

John Chrysostom gives a good explanation of the reasons why we sometimes do not obtain what we have asked for: 'is there any place where two are of one accord? Yes, in many places, or rather, surely everywhere. Why then, you may object, do they not obtain everything they ask for?

'There are many reasons which prevent their receiving what they requested. Often they ask things that are not useful or fitting . . . Others are not up to the level [of asking] . . . . In fact, Jesus looks for people who are similar to the apostles. For this reason he says, "if two of you agree . . ." that is, of you who practise virtue and live a life according to the Gospel.

'Again others pray against those who have offended them, calling down punishment and vengeance, and this has been forbidden by a precise commandment: "Pray for your enemies." [cf. Matt. 5:44]

'Finally some people ask God for mercy without however repenting for their sins . . .

'But if all the conditions called for are present, that is, if you ask fitting things, if you do all your part, if you live a life like that of the apostles, if you have unity of thought with your neighbours and love them, you will obtain what you ask for. For the Lord indeed is good and merciful.'[176]

We have observed that the consenserint has a great advantage: it prevents pride, which is almost inevitable in us poor human beings, when we obtain what we have asked for. And this is so because we know that with the consenserint not only is it Christ in our midst who is asking, but also it is not we alone who ask.

Listen to how well Athanasius of Sinai explains this idea: 'The Lord, who knows well the various thoughts and the pride of humanity, wants us not to have trust in ourselves, no matter how much we may lead a life dedicated to virtue and sanctity, but rather wants that, when we ask something, we hold our selves to be unworthy of obtaining what we wish for, and therefore we unite ourselves to others who think and feel in the same way as we do.

'In fact, someone who prays and obtains on his or her own often becomes proud; whereas we remain within the limits of humility if there is more than one who prays and obtains.'[177]

The focolare, the other forms of life in the Ideal, the little towns which repeat in the twentieth century the historical forms of religious life that have added splendour to the Church through the course of time, and the consenserint, a prayer which is infallible if there are all the required conditions, these are the topics I am dealing with today. May God make us more and more worthy of such a high vocation, and may he fill our hands with graces to distribute in a world that is cold and arid, a world that does not know what it means to live in relationship with a father who would like to give once again to all the presence of his own Son, and along with him, many, many graces.

Jesus in the Midst in the History of the Church

In the three preceding conversations it was almost as if we wanted to question the Fathers of the Church, fully aware of their competency in order to console ourselves concerning the understanding the Lord had given us about his words. 'Where two or three are gathered together in my name, I am there among them'

The Fathers, I think, have answered generously.

Jesus in the midst and the saints

Now the question that comes to mind is this: was it only the Fathers who spoke so explicitly about Jesus in the midst? A study could be made in depth of all the history of the Church.

We can reply that, when we read the lives of the saints, for example, we have often found these words of Jesus emphasized in various circumstances, and this is what has happened to me in the past months.

The Venerable Bede, who is also a Father of the Church, is so filled with these words that he has them in mind when he writes his commentary on the passage of Luke's Gospel: 'As they were saying this, Jesus himself stood among them, and said to them, "Peace be with you: fear not, it is I."' (cf. Luke 24:36) Bede says:

'The first thing to note in this passage and to remember carefully, is that God deigned to be present in the midst of the disciples who were talking about him, and to reveal his presence by letting them see him. This, in fact, is the same thing that he had promised in another instance to all his disciples: "Where two or three are gathered together in my name, there am I in the midst of them." Indeed, in order to confirm our faith, at times he wanted to appear also in a bodily way, just as he always shows himself through the presence of his divine love. Although we may be much inferior to the apostles, we must, in fact, believe that through his mercy the same thing happens for us too. That is, he is in the midst of us each time we meet together in his name.'[178]

Sometimes we feel like asking ourselves, if we consider the great light that we feel has overwhelmed us in these past thirty three years, what testament we would like to leave to those who follow the same path as us. Without a doubt our choice would be the very testament of Jesus: mutual love and unity, which bring the presence of Jesus in the midst.

Only by leaving behind us this presence of Jesus in every corner of the world where the Movement lives can we be certain that everything will carry on for the best, and that he will continue to be teacher, guide, father, and leader of each group of persons, whether small or large, which has him among its members. He alone will be capable of fulfilling the Work of Mary according to the plan kept in his heart.

In the testament of Angela Merici, I found some marvellous

pages where unity is the most outstanding note: 'especially take care,' she writes, 'that [my daughters] be united and in agreement in all they desire, as we read of the apostles and of the Christians of the early Church: *Erat autem eorum cor unum* ... And you, too, try to be this way with all your daughters, because the more you are united, the more Jesus Christ will be in your midst as a father and good shepherd.

'With these my final words to you, I plead even to my dying breath that you be in harmony, united together, all one heart and one will. Be bound to one another in the bond of charity, esteeming one another, helping one another, putting up with one another in Jesus Christ. Because if you try to be like this, without a doubt the Lord God will be in your midst ...

'Therefore, see how important this union and concord is. Desire it, seek it out, embrace it, hold fast to it with all your might: because I tell you that if you are all together thus united in heart, you will be like a very strong fortress or an invincible tower in the face of every adversity, persecution or diabolical trickery. Moreover, I tell you that every grace that you ask of God will unfailingly be granted.'[179]

We have already mentioned that prayer in common is superior to individual prayer. The Curé D'Ars said that in the evening, before going to bed, it is necessary to pray together, because 'If two or three persons unite together to pray in my name, I will be in the midst of them.'[180]

Also Thérèse of Lisieux wrote: 'I dearly love prayer in common, because Jesus promised to "be present in the midst of those who meet together in his name;" and so I feel that the fervour of my sisters makes up for what is lacking in mine.'[181]

She also says: 'united in him our souls will be able to save many other souls, because our sweet Jesus said: "If two of you agree on earth about anything they ask, it will be done for them."'[182]

In the Movement, whenever we meet together to speak about our great Ideal, we usually start out by stating a condition, or better by trying to create a certain reality: we invite everybody present to put aside every personal problem so as to be ready to obtain, all together, the presence of Jesus in the midst. Only after having done this, and never before, does the meeting begin.

When Don Bosco called the first General Chapter of the Holy Society of Salesians, which was held in Lanzo near Turin in 1877, he began by saying: 'Our Divine Saviour says in the Gospel that where two or three are gathered together in his name there he is in the midst of them. We have no other aim in our meeting than the glory of God, and the salvation of souls redeemed by the precious blood of Jesus Christ. Therefore we can be certain that the Lord will be in our midst and will manage things in such a way as to bring about great good.'[183]

Jesus in the midst and the Councils of the Church

But there is a great event, the greatest event, which every so often takes place in the Church: an Ecumenical Council. It is not of divine institution, but, 'nevertheless' writes Yves Congar, 'in the Council there is a certain structure to which the Lord freely united his presence with a formal promise: "I am with you always, to the end of the age", "Where two or three are gathered together in my name, I am there among them.".... '

'In this we find a structure of the covenant (people meet together in the name of Jesus – Jesus becomes present in their midst) comparable on its own level with that other structure which is more of an institutional form, that is to say, more of a juridical form, the structure of the covenant constituted by the sacraments or by the hierarchical ministries.

'This is exactly how the Fathers of the Church understood it. According to them once these conditions have been fulfilled and these structures of the covenant are respected, in other words once there is fraternal love and the fraternal meeting of two or three in his name, then the Lord carries out his promise, which is effectively bound up with these conditions,'[184] that is, he becomes present.

The Fathers, in fact, tenaciously maintain that Jesus is present in the midst of Bishops in the Councils. As a result the Council ends up being like the great 'focolare' of the Church where Jesus extends his light abundantly in order to enlighten the centuries to come.

Cyril of Alexandria says: 'Those well-known Fathers of ours who met one day in Nicea and defined the venerable and universal Symbol of Faith, also tried to follow in the footsteps of the Apostles. Certainly together with them sat Christ himself, Christ who said: "Where two or three are gathered together in my name, there am I in the midst of them."

'How could anyone doubt that Christ invisibly presided over that great and Holy Synod? In fact it laid throughout the entire world a firm and unshakeable foundation: the confession of the true, blameless faith. If this is true, how could Christ have been absent, since he himself is its foundation, as the wise words of Paul indicate".'[185] That is, 'For no one can lay any foundation other than the one that has been laid; that foundation is Jesus Christ.' (1 Cor. 3:11)

John Chrysostom, writing to a Jew advises: 'Be careful of what you are doing when you condemn such illustrious Fathers [of the Council of Nicea], such strong, wise Fathers. . .

'Do you not know the words of Christ: "Where two or three are gathered together in my name, there am I in the midst of them"? Because, if where there are two or three Christ is in their midst, with all the more reason where there were three hundred and many more, he was present and he disposed and decided everything.'[186]

The same applies to every true focolare where we are certain that it is he who decides and plans everything. In fact, we do not feel we are doing the will of a man or a woman when we are given some task, but the will of Jesus in the midst, and this creates in us a sense of the freedom of the children of God.

Leontius writes: 'There in the Council, you say, a few people were present whom it is well known once favoured Nestorius . . .

'How . . . because of the presence of two or three unfortunate members who, unknown to the others have impious thoughts, could the entire venerable assembly and the sacred synod of holy prelates, almost as if they were all impious, be abandoned by God and thus be unable to discern the truth, especially when God himself promised: "Where two or three are gathered together in my name, there am I in the midst of them."'[187]

And John of Damascus writes: 'Regarding these matters the decision does not rest with emperors, but with the Councils, just as our Lord said: "Where two or three are gathered together in my name, there am I in the midst of them."'[188]

And is it not consoling for us, and encouraging that the greatest event of the Church has the structure that God gave to us little children of the Church? How beautiful and consoling it is to mirror ourselves in such a mother.

Jesus in the midst in the Second Vatican Council

Let us now take a look at the Second Vatican Council, which God willed should take place during our lifetime.

It, too, was certainly guided by Jesus in the midst of the Fathers. But since for us, who live in this century, it is extremely important to see whether the charism that inspires us is in agreement with the spirit of the entire present-day Church, let us look through the pages of the Council documents to see if the Council speaks explicitly about Jesus in the midst.

Yes, it does. In fact Pasquale Foresi in his book *God Among Men* says: 'Until Vatican II the phrase of the Gospel "Where two or three have met together in my name, I am there among them" was rarely mentioned. In the entire history of the Church, with the exception of the Council of Chalcedon,[189] it was hardly ever quoted in important conciliar documents. Whereas at Vatican II not a document overlooked this fundamental idea . . . this idea of course was, the soul of the Council, above all in the *Decree on the Pastoral Office of Bishops in the Church*[190].'[191]

Vatican II mentions Jesus in the midst in the *Constitution on the Sacred Liturgy*. After having enumerated the various ways

Christ is present in the life of the Church it says: 'Lastly, he is present when the Church prays and sings, for he has promised "where two or three are gathered together in my name, there am I in the midst of them".'[192]

We find Jesus in the midst mentioned in a splendid way in the *Decree on the Renewal of Religious Life*. When we read this passage we understand why the branch of the religious, men and women, had to come to life from the Work of Mary. The charism that God gave us is brimming over with these ideas, with these truths. Therefore, our charism can be helpful to many religious who may not know how to put these words of the Council into practice or who, in times of religious crisis as at present, may have lost their understanding of the religious life.

'Common life, in prayer and the sharing of the same spirit (Acts 2:42) should be constant, after the example of the early Church, in which the company of believers were of one heart and soul. It should be nourished by the teaching of the Gospel and by the sacred liturgy, especially by the eucharist. Religious, as members of Christ, should live together as brothers and should give pride of place to one another in esteem (cf. Rom. 12:10), carrying one another's burdens (cf. Gal. 6:12). A community gathered together as a true family in the Lord's name enjoys his presence (cf. Matt. 18:20) through the love of God which is poured into their hearts by the Holy Spirit (cf. Rom. 5:5). For love sums up the law (cf. Rom. 13:10) and is the bond which makes us perfect (cf. Col. 3:14); by it we know that we have crossed over from death to life (cf. 1 John 3:14). Indeed, the unity of the brethren is a symbol of the coming of Christ (cf. John 13:35; 17:21) and is a source of great apostolic power.'[193]

The Second Vatican Council speaks about Jesus in the midst again in the *Decree on the Apostolate of the Laity*, when it speaks of the apostolate of individuals saying that it is useful above all in those places where the Church is hampered, and suggesting in any case that they, 'can gather for discussion into small groups with no rigid form of rules or organization . . . It ensures the continual presence before the eyes of others of a sign of the Church's community, a sign that will be seen as a genuine witness of love.'[194]

Then in speaking about group apostolate, it emphasizes the line of action that God gave to our Movement too. After having affirmed that 'where two or three are gathered together in my name, I am there among them,' it says: 'For that reason Christians will exercise their apostolate in a spirit of concord.'[195]

In this same decree, of the principal fields of apostolic activity, the first to be mentioned is the parish, which 'offers an outstanding example of community apostolate' and the second is the family.[196]

I feel I want to stop here to praise God for having led us to found the New Parish Movement and the New Family Movement.

Is it not clear that it is Jesus in the midst who leads us on, that same Jesus who presided over the recent Council?

Finally, the Council speaks about Jesus in the midst in the *Decree on Ecumenism*, inviting all believers, in order to bring about the union of Christians, to lead a life according to the Gospel and to use the consenserint to beseech the grace of unity 'for where two or three are gathered together in my name, there am I in the midst of them.'[197] In this aspect, too, we feel that our vocation is surprisingly up-to-date. Through our effort to live the Gospel we are in line; not being able to be united with most of the separated Churches in the Eucharist, we feel we can be united, when the necessary conditions are fulfilled, by the presence of Jesus among two or more. This is our ecumenism.

Jesus in the midst in the teaching of Pope Paul VI

To conclude, let us see if Pope Paul has made mention of Jesus in the midst.

To our knowledge he has, and more than once. He has mentioned Jesus in the midst in his address to the Cardinals in the 1969 Consistory; to the Italian Episcopal Conference; to the Parish Priests and Lenten preachers of Rome, and on other occasions.

A splendid example is what we heard the Pope say on the occasion of his visit to the Parish of Mary, Comforter of the Afflicted: 'Are the faithful united in love, in the charity of Christ? Then certainly this is a living parish, here is the true Church, since the divine and human phenomenon which perpetuates the presence of Christ among us is flourishing. Or are the faithful together only because they are registered in the Parish Register or in the list of those who have been baptized? Are they together only because they meet on Sundays to hear Mass, without knowing one another, maybe even pushing into one another? If this is so, the Church in this case does not appear bound together; the cement, which must make all members into a real, organic unity, is not yet at work . . .

'Remember,' the Pope concludes, 'those solemn words of Christ. They will truly recognize you as my disciples, as authentic faithful followers, if you love one another, if there is this warmth of affection, of feelings; if love for others is alive, more a willed love than a sentiment, more something that we have created than something spontaneous, with that openness of heart and that capacity of generating Christ in our midst which derives exactly from our feeling that we are united in him and through him.'[198]

If the 'true Church' is like this, we must say that everything invites our Movement to exert the maximum effort, to make this Church shine out in as many places as possible with the presence of Jesus among us.

References

The Word Of Life

1. Augustine, *Homilies on John*, 106, in *A library of the Fathers of the Catholic Church*, London 1883, vol. 2, p. 967.
2. *Works of St. Justin Martyr in the Oxford Library of the Fathers*, Oxford 1861, *Dialogue with Trypho* 8, p.81.
3. St Gregory, PG 37, 1553A *Poemata as alios VII (ad Nemesium)*, vv. 37-49.
4. St Basil, *The Letters*, Loeb Classical Library, vol. 3, London 1962, CCXXIII, p. 293.
5. St Justin, *II Apologia pro Christianis*, 10, PG 6, 459 B.
6. St Justin, *Dialogue with Trypho* 8, op. cit., p.81.
7. Thérèse of Lisieux, *Autobiography of a Saint*, London 1958, p. 218.
8. *The Way of Perfection* XXI, *The Complete Works of St. Teresa*, London 1946, vol. 2, p. 90.
9. *Obras de san Buenaventura*, BAC, Madrid 1957, vol. III, p. 541.
10. *Exercises of St. Gertrude the Great OSB*, Badia di Praglia 1924, Ex. V, pp. 106ff.
11. Hilary of Poitiers, *Tract. in Psalmum* 13, PL 9, 295 A.
12. Maximus of Turin, *Sermon 105* PL 57, 740 D (*de calice aquae frigidae*).
13. Bernard of Clairvaux, *De Tempore*, 'In Septuagesima', First sermon, 2 PL 183, 163C.
14. *Letter to St Eusebius in Matt.*, PL 26, 93 A-C.
15. *Sermon 120*, 2-3 PL 38, 677.
16. *De oratione dominica*, 1-2 PL 4, 537 A.
17. *Homilies on Matthew by John Chrysostom XVI 5, Library of the Fathers of the Holy Catholic Church, anterior to the division of East and West*, vol. 1, London 1883, p. 232.

[18] St Clement, *Second letter to the Corinthians, 13, Library of Christian Classics*, vol. 1, London 1953, p. 198.

[19] *Homilies on the Gospel according to St John LXXXI 4, Library of the Fathers of the Holy Catholic Church, anterior to the division of East and West*, London 1883, vol. 2, p. 831-32..

[20] *De Abraham*, lib II, 22, PL 14, 488 A.

[21] *Straomatics*, 1, 1.

[22] *Ignatius to the Philadelphians*, 5, PG 5, 699 C, London 1946, p.86.

[23] *In Ecclesiastes*, 3, 13 PL 23, 1039 A.

[24] *Sermo 300 (qualiter excipiendum sit Dei Verbum)*, 2-3, PL 39, 2319.

[25] *Dei Verbum 21, Documents of Vatican II*, London 1967, p.125.

[26] *In Psalmum* 118, 50, PG 27, 487 D.

[27] Discourse (for Lent) 27.2.66).

[28] St Gregory the Great, *The Books of the Monks, Library of the Fathers of the Holy Catholic Church, anterior to the division East and West*, Oxford 1844, Book VI, 22, p. 327

[29] *Expos. in Psalmum 39*, 16, PL 14, 114 C.

[30] *Commentary on the Gospel of St. John*, XL, I, from *Commento al Vangelo di San Giovanni*, Città Nuova, Rome 1965, vol. II, p. 2.

[31] *De Abraham*, Book II, 22, PL 14, 483 A.

[32] John of Damascus, *Exposition of the Orthodox Faith*, IV, 17, p.89, Oxford 1899.

[33] *Hom. de capto Eutropio et de divitiarum vanitate*, 1, PG 52. 395.

[34] *Tractatus asceticus*, c. 5, PL 158, 1033 C.

[35] Extract from speech by Pope Paul VI to the parish of S. Eusebio, 26.2.67.

[36] Ignatius to the Romans in *Early Christian Fathers*, OUP 1969, p. 45.

[37] Gregory the Great, *Hom. in ev.*, referred to by Bede, *Commentary on the Gospel of St. Mark, (Found in Commento al*

Vangelo di S. Marco, Città Nuova, Rome 1970, Vol. I, p. 116-117).
38 Augustine, *Homilies on the Psalms*, Psalm 45: 8, *Library of the Holy Catholic Church, anterior to the division East and West*, Oxford 1948, vol. II, p. 251.
39 Clement of Alexandria, vol. 2, p. 482, Edinburgh 1869.
40 In Commentary on the Song of Songs, Sermon 1, PG 44, 778D.

The Eucharist

41 Thérèse of Lisieux, *Manuscrits autobiographiques*, manuscrit 'B' deuxieme partie, Lisieux, 1957. Cf. *Autobiography of a Saint*, trans. Ronald Knox, Harvill Press, London, 1958, p. 241.
42 Pierre Julien Eymard, *La Sainte Eucharistie*, La Presence Reelle, Tome 1, Paris, 1949, p. 87.
43 Cf. The Office of Corpus Christi, Lesson IV, Old Roman Breviary.
44 Pierre Julien Eymard, ibid., p. 142.
45 Ignatius of Antioch, *Ephesians* 19, 1 (PG 5, 660) *Library of Christian Classics*, Vol. 1, trans. and ed. C.C. Richardson, SCM, London 1953, p.93.
46 'Decree on the Ministry and Life of Priests' (*Presbyterorum Ordinis*) 5 in Vatican Council 11, *The Conciliar and Post Conciliar Documents*, ed. Austin Flannery OP, Dominican Publications, Dublin 1975, p. 871.
47 Cf J. Castellano, *Eucaristia* in DES 1, Rome 1975, p. 737.
48 *Insegnamenti di Paolo VI*, Poliglotta Vaticana, 1967, IV, p. 164.
49 Pierre Benoit, cited in Castellano, ibid., p. 738.
50 Athanasius, *Letter IV*, 3. Easter Day. For 332 in *A Select Library of Nicene and Post-Nicene Fathers*, Vol. IV, ed. Archibald Robertson, Parker & Co., Oxford 1892 (PG 26, 1377), p. 516.
51 Ibid.

52. Cf ibid., IV, 5 (PG 26, 1379), p. 517.
53. Albert the Great, *De Euch.*, d. 1, c. 2, n. 7 (Borgnet edition, Vol. 38, p. 200)
54. John Chrysostom, *In I Cor., hom. 24*, 2 (PG 61, 200) in *A Library of Fathers of the Holy Catholic Church*, Oxford 1884, p. 327-8.
55. Justin, *First Apology* 1, 67, 65 (PG 6, 429-32, 427), in *Library of Christian Classics*, Vol. 1, SCM, London 1953, pp. 285-6, 287.
56. Ibid., 1, 66 (PG 6, 427), in op. cit., p. 286.
57. Ibid., in op. cit..
58. *Didache* 9, 4, in *Library of Christian Classics*, Vol. I, op. cit., p. 175.
59. Ignatius of Antioch, *Smyrnaeans*, 8, 1 (PG 5, 713ff), in op. cit., p.115.
60. Quoted in J. Quasten, *Patrology*, Vol. 1, Spectrum, Utrecht 1950, p. 78.
61. Irenaeus, *Against the Heresies*, IV, 18, 5 (PG 7, 1027) in *Ante-Nicene Christian Library*, Vol. 5, T & T Clark, Edinburgh 1868, p. 435.
62. For this section and the two following, cf. J. Castellano, op. cit., p. 741-45.
63. Cf. *St Michael's Daily Missal*, Goodliffe Neale, Alcester & Dublin 1973, p. 340-58.
64. Quoted in Paul IV's *Mysterium Fidei*, Encyclical on the Holy Eucharist, C.T.S., London 1965, no. 45, p. 20. Cf. Council of Trent, *Decree on the Eucharist*, Chap. 1.
65. *Mysterium Fidei* no. 27, pp. 12-13 in Trent, *Doctrine of the Most Holy Sacrifice of the Mass*, ch. 1.
66. *The Constitution on the Sacred Liturgy*, 47-48 in *The Conciliar and Post Conciliar Documents*, op. cit., pp. 16-17.
67. *Messale della Domenica*, Rome 1973, pp. 441-2.
68. Thomas Aquinas, *Summa theologiae* III, q 79, q 1, Blackfriars, 1975, Vol. 59, p. 5.

69 Thomas Aquinas, *Commentary on the Gospel of John* 6:54.
70 Thomas Aquinas, *Commentary on 1 Cor.*, c. 11, 1, 5.
71 Cf. Yves Congar - P. Rossano, *Proprietà essenziali della Chiesa in Myst.* Sal. VII, Brescia 1972, pp. 469-71.
72 'The Constitution of the Church' (*Lumen Gentium*) 26 in *The Conciliar and Post Conciliar Documents*, op. cit., p. 382, quoting Leo the Great, *Serm.* 63,7 (PL 54, 357C).
73 Thomas Aquinas, *In Sent.* IV, dist 12, q 2, a 1.
74 Cyril of Jerusalem, *Cat. Myst.* 4, 3 (PG 33, 1100) in *The Fathers of the Church*, Vol. 64, 'The Works of St Cyril of Jerusalem' trs. L. P. McCauley SJ & A. A. Stephenson. The Catholic University America, Washington 1970, pp. 181-2.
75 Ibid., p. 182.
76 Leo the Great, *Serm.* (PL 54, 357C).
77 Augustine, *Confessions*, Vll 10 (PL 32, 742) ed. & trs. R. S. Pine-Coffin, Penguin 1971, p. 147.
78 Albert the Great, *De Euch.*, D.3 tr 1, c. 5, Borgnet edition, Vol. 38, p. 257
79 Albert the Great, *In IV Sent.* D. 9, a. 2 (Borgnet 29), p. 217.
80 Albert the Great, *De Euch.*, D.3, tr. l, c. 8, n.2 (Borgnet 38), p. 272.
81 Ibid.
82 Ibid.
83 Thérèse of Lisieux, *Manuscrits autobiographiques*, op cit. manuscrit 'A', p. 83. Knox trs. op. cit., p. 106.
84 Anselm Stoltz OSB, *Theologie der Mystik*, Regensburg 1936; *The Doctrine of Spiritual Perfection*, trs. A. Williams OSB, B. Herder, London 1938, pp. 228-9.
85 Carmel de Lisieux, 'Mon ciel a moi' in *Poesies de Sainte Thérèse de l'Enfant-Jesus*, Office central de Lisieux, 1951, p. 31.
86 Carmel de Lisieux, 'Le petit mendiant de Noel', ibid., p. 105.
87 Pierre Julien Eymard, op. cit., pp. 303-5.
88 Irenaeus, *Against the Heresies (Adv. haer.)*, V, 2, 3 (PG 7 1124),

op. cit., Library of Christian Classics, Vol. 1, SCM, London 1953, pp. 388-9.

[89] D. van den Eynde, *L'Eucaristia in S. Ignazio, S. Giustino e S. Ireneo in Eucaristia*, ed. A. Piolanti, Rome 1957, p. 120.

[90] Origen, *Prayer (De orat.)* 27, 9 in *Ancient Christian Writers*, Vol. XIX trs. J. J. O'Meara, Longmans, Green & Co., London 1954, p. 99.

[91] Thomas Aquinas, *Commentary on the Gospel of John* 6:55.

[92] *L'Osservatore Romano*, English edition, April 22, 1976, p. 1, columns 2 & 3.

[93] *The Constitution on the Church*, 50, *The Conciliar and Post Conciliar Documents*, op. cit., p. 412.

[94] John of Damascus, *De Fide Orthodoxa* IV, 13 (PG 94, 1154) in *A Select Library of Nicene and Post-Nicene Fathers of the Christian Church*, Vol. IX, trs. S. D. F. Salmon, Oxford 1899, p. 84.

[95] P. Jacquimont, *Origene in L'Eucharistie chez les premiers chrétiens*, Paris 1976, p. 181.

[96] Albert the Great, *In Jo.* 6, 64 (Borgnet 24, 288).

[97] Albert the Great, *De Oe. Hierarch.* 3, 2 (Borgnet 14, 561).

[98] Albert the Great, IV Sent., d. 8, a. 11 (Borgnet 29, 206).

[99] Cf. *De Euch.* d. 3, trs. 2, c. 5. n. 5 (Borgnet 38, 300).

[100] *Insegnamenti di Paolo VI*, Poliglotta Vaticana, 1966, Vol. III, p. 358.

[101] *Didache*, 9.5 and 14, 1-2, op. cit., pp. 175 & 178.

[102] Justin, *First Apology*, 1, 66 (PG 6, 427) op. cit., p. 64.

[103] John Chrysostom, *In Matth.* hom 82,4. (PG 58, 743 f), cf. *The Homilies of St John Chrysostom on the Gospel of St Matthew*, part III, Oxford 1885, pp. 1090-91.

[104] Origen, *In Matth. comm.* 10, 25 (PG 13, 904) in *The Ante-Nicene Fathers*, Vol. X, New York 1925, p. 431.

[105] Cyprian, *De oratione dominica*, 23 (PL 4, 535) in *The Fathers of the Church*, Vol. 36, New York 1958, p. 148.

[106] John Chrysostom, *De Prod. Judae* 1, 6 (PG 49, 380-82).

[107] Ignatius of Antioch, *Smyrnaeans* 9, 1 (PG 5, 713f) in *Library of Christian Classics*, Vol. 1, SCM, London 1953, p. 115.

[108] Albert the Great, *De Euch.*, d. 3, tr. 4, c. 3 (Borgnet 38, 325).

[109] Thomas Aquinas, *Commentary on the Gospel of John*, 6, 57.

[110] *Insegnamenti di Paolo VI*, Poliglotta Vaticana, 1967, IV, p. 288.

[111] Thomas Aquinas, *Summa theologiae*, III q.79, a.6, ad. 3 op. cit., p.23.

[112] Catherine of Siena as cited in *Il Messaggio di Santa Caterina da Siena Dottore della Chiesa*, Rome 1970, pp. 646-8.

[113] Paul of the Cross, *Scritti Spirituali*, Città Nuova, 1974, p. 39.

[114] Sacred Congregation of Rites, *Decree on Eucharistic Mystery*, 38.

[115] J. Castellano, op. cit., p. 750.

[116] *Insegnamenti di Paolo VI*, Poliglotta Vaticana, 1969, VI, p. 389.

[117] E. Mersch, *The Theology of the Mystical Body*, trs. C. Vollert SJ, London 1958, pp. 592-93.

[118] Cf Cyprian, op. cit., p. 148.

[119] *Insegnamenti di Paolo VI*, Poliglotta Vaticana, 1967 Vol. IV, p. 288.

[120] Ibid., 1966, Vol. III, pp. 358-9.

[121] Ibid., 1969, Vol. VI, p. 249.

[122] Cf. F. Durrwell, *L'Eucharistie, presence du Christ*, Paris 1971, pp. 44-6.

[123] Cyril of Jerusalem, *Cat. Myst.* 5, 7 (PG 33 1113) op. cit., p. 196.

[124] J. Betz *L'Eucaristia come mistero centrale* in *Myst. Sal.*, Vol. VIII, Brescia 1975, p. 261.

[125] 'Decree on Ecumenism', (*Unitatis Redintegratio*), 15, *The Conciliar and Post Conciliar Documents*, op. cit., p. 465

Where Two or Three

[126] *Selecta in Jer.*, 23, 23. PG 13, 57I

[127] *Demonstr. evang.*, lib. 5, 26. PG 22, 406-7.

[128] *Comment. in Psalm*, 84. PG 23, 1003-6.

[129] *Hom.in Isa*, 6,2, PG 56, 137.
[130] *Contra Celsum*, 2,9, PG 11,810.
[131] *Hom. in. Isa.*, 1,5, PG 13, 223-24.
[132] *In. Jo. evang.*, 9, PG 74, 155.
[133] *Comment. in Matt.*, 14, 1ff., PG I3, 1191.
[134] *Enarr. in evang. Matth.*, 18, 19-20, PG 123, 343
[135] *De exhort. cast.*, PL 2, 971.
[136] *Pal. trans. liber.*, PG 152, 702.
[137] *Comment. in Psalm*, 46, PG 23, 422.
[138] *Comment. in Isa.*, 19, PG 24, 222.
[139] *Constit. Apost.*, 8, 34, PG 1, 1138.
[140] *De Fuga*, 14, PL 2, 142.
[141] *Sermones catech.*, PG 99, 622.
[142] *Epist. fest.*, 10, 2, PG 26, 1397-8.
[143] That is, the spirituality of unity as lived by the members of the Focolare Movement.
[144] *De Eccl. unit.*, 12, PL 4, 524-5.
[145] *In Eccle.*, 4, PG 98, 914.
[146] *Practic. capit.*, 1. PG 120, 887.
[147] *Expos. in Psalm 133*, PG 55, 385.
[148] *In Epist. ad Hebr.* 10, 25. Hom. 19,1, PG 63, 140.
[149] *In Inscript. Act. Apost.*, 2, 4, PG 51, 83.
[150] *Reg. brevius tract.*, Interr. 255, PG 31, 1231.
[151] *Hom. in Matth.* 60, 3, PG 58, 587.
[152] *Epist.* 2. PG 99, 1350.
[153] *Comment. in Matth.* 14, 1 s., PG 13, 1187.
[154] *Comm. al Cantico*, 41, PG 13, 94B.
[155] *Comment. in Matth.* 14, 1 s., PG 13, 1183-86.
[156] Ibid. PG 13, 1186.
[157] *Orat.* 42, *Supremum vale*, PG 36, 467.
[158] The Genfest is organized by the young people of the Focolare Movement. It is an international event that shows through music, dance, mime, talks and the sharing of real life experi-

ences what it means to live the Gospel.
159. *Address by Pope Paul VI to the New Generation Movement* (that is, the Gen, young people of the Focolare Movement), 2 March 1975. *Osservatore Romano* –English Weekly Edition, No. 11., 13 March 1975.
160. *Comment. in Matth.* 13, 15, PG 13, 1131.
161. Ibid.
162. *De Anna*, Sermo 5, 1, PG 54, 669.
163. *Expos. in Proph. Os.*, PG 126, 587.
164. A focolare is a small community of men or women who live the spirituality of the Focolare Movement.
165. *In can.* 17, Conc. oecum. 7, PG 137, 974.
166. *De monast. laic. non trad.*, PG 132, 1134.
167. *Vita S. Gregorii theologi*, PG 35, 259.
168. *Reg. fusius tract.*, Interr. 5, 3, PG 31, 923.
169. *Reg. fusius tract.*, Interr. 37, 4, PG 31, 1014.
170. Epist. 97
171. *Constit. ascet.* 34,1, PG 31, 1423-26.
172. *Epist.*, lib. 2, PG 99, 1446.
173. *In Epist. 2 ad Thess.* Hom. 4,4, PG 62, 491.
174. Cf. Peter Chrysologus, *Sermo 132*, PL 52, 56.
175. Ibid. PL 52, 562.
176. *Hom In Matth.*, 60, 2.
177. *Quaest.*, PG 89, 762-63.
178. *Hom.*, 2, 9, CCL 122, 240.
179. Teresa Ledóchowska OSU, *Il Ceppo dai molti virgulti*, Milan 1972, pp. 187-8.
180. *Scritti Scelti* (Selected Writings), Rome 1975, p. 44.
181. *Gli Scritti* (Collected Writings), Rome 1970, p. 289.
182. Op. cit., pp. 712-3.
183. G. B. Lemoyne, *Vita di S. Giovanni Bosco*, Turin 1962,Vol. 2. p. 140.
184. *Note sul concilio come assemblea e sulla conciliarità fondamentale della*

[185]   Chiesa, in *Orizzonti attuali della teologia*, Rome 1967, Vol. 2. pp. 172-3.
[185]   *Epist.* 55, PG 77, 294.
[186]   *Adv. Jud. orat.*, 3. PG 48, 865.
[187]   *Contra Monoph.*, PG 86, 1878.
[188]   *De imag.*, orat 1. PG 94, 1282.
[189]   Cf. PL 54, 959.
[190]   *Lumen Gentium*. 3
[191]   *God Among Men*, London 1974, p. 50.
[192]   *Constitution Sacrosanctum Concilium*, 1, 7. in *The Conciliar and Post Conciliar Documents*, op. cit., p.5.
[193]   *Perfectae caritatis*, 15 in *The Conciliar and Post Conciliar Documents*, ibid., p. 620.
[194]   *Apostolicam Actuositatem*, 4, 18 in *The Conciliar and Post Conciliar Documents*, ibid., p.785.
[195]   Ibid.
[196]   Ibid., cf. sections 9, 10, 11.
[197]   *Unitatis Redintegratio*, 2, 8, ibid., p. 461.
[198]   *Insegnamenti di Paola VI*, Poliglotta Vaticana, Vatican City. 1965 Vol. 2. pp. 1072-74.